THE LITURGY OF THE LAND

Cultivating a Catholic Homestead

THE LITURGY
OF THE LAND

Cultivating a Catholic Homestead

Jason M. Craig & Thomas D. Van Horn

TAN Books
Gastonia, North Carolina

Cover and interior design by David Ferris, www.davidferrisdesign.com.

Cover Image by Oksana Bondartsuk/Shutterstock.com.
Interior photography by Andrew Gwynn and Carrie Allen.

ISBN: 978-1-5051-2832-1
Kindle ISBN: 978-1-5051-2906-9
ePUB ISBN: 978-1-5051-2907-6

Published in the United States by
TAN Books
PO Box 269
Gastonia, NC 28053
www.TANBooks.com

Printed in India

CONTENTS

It seems that most families have an "agrarian moment" at some point. It happens when they dream of their family living on a farm, growing food, working together, slowing down, unplugging, and enjoying such a life with others. They see children in the yard feeding chickens, mothers in the garden checking on what is ripe for the table, and the father coming back from the field, perhaps discussing the day's work with an older son in celebratory satisfaction, sharing work, responsibility, and care for the same place with one another. They see themselves working hard but closer to home and closer to each other.

Often, people that find themselves longing for life on the land are serious in their faith because they find something in their modern way of life that, at best, makes it difficult to live their faith and, at worst, is inherently opposed to it. In fact, many budding agrarians point to their faith as the very thing "driving" them to the land.

In *The Liturgy of the Land,* our proposal is that while it is possible to romanticize the life of homesteading to the point of sentimentalized caricatures of reality, it is also true that homesteading is romanticized because it is romantic. The family homestead is not simply a different *option* among others, as if life is nothing but a series of lifestyle choices, but it is the *natural* place and work that lends itself uniquely to growth in virtue and holiness. In short, life on a homestead is good because it brings us closer to our family, to nature, and to our local community. Yet, the greatest motivation to take up this lifestyle is that homesteading can help orient us more fully and simply toward our true and lasting happiness, which is God Himself.

AN OLDISH WORD

To better understand what we mean by a Catholic homestead, we might consider why we use that word in the subtitle and not "farm."

The word "homestead" originates from the Old English word *hamsted,* which could refer to a specific home or even a village. "Home" obviously refers to the dwelling of a family, and the old word *stead* referred to a place that was firm and established; think of *stead* with another related word, "steady." A homestead is a place where a family is rooted in the use or ownership of a piece of land.

American usage, however, has given the word staying power, as it referred to the various homesteading acts of the federal government that launched people out—especially in the westward expansion of the United States—to establish themselves on newly claimed or conquered lands. Wrapped up in this history, homesteading has some mixed realities for us today, but its roots are deeper than one nation's history because the homesteaders then were mostly looking for the same thing they are today—even if the realities look very different.

In both Old and American English, therefore, we see that a homestead is not merely a property used to grow crops but a piece of land defined by the presence of a rooted family. Also, contrary to charges of isolationism, the connection to words defined as "village" reminds us that Catholic families rooted in the land always grow outward into communal life, hopefully and most ideally with other Catholics, so that the community can meet both physical and spiritual needs. The land is also utilized primarily for the purpose of providing for that family in a manner usually called *subsistence,* which means the agricultural effort is oriented toward the life of the family itself and, therefore, the family is oriented toward the life of the farm. The union of the family and the land is sacred, naturally mimicking the fruitful love of man that, when true and lasting, is fruitful and life-giving.

A CATHOLIC HOMESTEAD

If it is the family that makes a piece of land a homestead, it is the true Faith that makes the homestead Catholic. Our Faith is not merely a sort of religious branding that surrounds the practical work of the land; rather, it guides and sanctifies our work. We don't just pray our work goes well, but the work itself becomes actual prayer. Our Faith is the very life of our homesteads, and the liturgy we work on our land is nurtured by and united with the liturgy at the altar. The teachings of our Faith shape how we approach and cultivate our land and homes. We often hear that you can't separate work and "real life" from Sunday Mass and your life of faith. The same is even more true when the liturgical seasons and the seasons of nature are more clearly united. The cultivation of faith and the cultivation of land are so easily intertwined that it becomes no mystery as to why Our Lord so often spoke in agricultural parables. The Kingdom of God truly is like a seed sown in good soil, and good soil reminds us of the Kingdom of God.

Most people know that our technology-loving, post-industrial society is new. For centuries upon centuries prior—literally from the beginning of time—the work common to most men the world over was finding, growing, securing, and preserving food. These acts were foundational for staying alive, but providing for bodily needs also grew into beautiful and intricate cultures where food wasn't just important for staying alive but for living a life. This is because we, as man, must provide food like the beasts, but our work builds up into culture because we have souls. Intertwined with and sanctified by the Church, the life of prayer, work, fasting, and feasting formed a single life, an integrated whole. In the vast countryside of Christendom, the work of God (worship) and the work of the land was the life of the people, a single life undivided.

This natural work of man could truly be called a liturgy, a Greek word that means "the work of the people." Liturgy is work done for others, with others. The liturgy of the Church, as we know, is the life of the spirit received in the body through earthen elements grown and gathered by the faithful and made holy by the clergy. There will always be a close link between the work of the land and the work of the altar since the latter cannot happen without the former—the farmer. It is man who, from the soil and by his work, brings forth the goods of the earth that become the sacraments, become heavenly things. The work of the land does not stop at keeping our bellies full but is literally taken up by God through the Church to bring us to heaven and heaven to us. This is why we entitled this *The Liturgy of the Land*, communicating the connection between our life working in nature and our life in God. This is the work particularly suited to the laity, to the family, and to Catholic communities. It is by the cultivation of nature that we are brought into proximity and intimacy with the cultivation of faith and virtue.

The root of the word "cultivate" (*cult* in English from the Latin *cultis*) holds together a sort of holy tension between heaven and earth, and it is the vocation of man—body and soul—to hold the two together. "Cult," in Latin, can refer to the worship of God *and* the work of the land. This dual-purposed work has even caused tension for theologians. In trying to put a word to the act of Christian worship in the liturgy, Saint Augustine described why he does not prefer the word *cultus*, which is where we get the word "cultivate": "The word 'cult' (*cultus*) by itself would not imply something due only to God. . . . This word is employed not only in respect of things which in a spirit of devout humility we regard above us, but even some things which are below us. For from the same word are derived *agriculae* (cultivators), *coloni* (farmers) and *incolae* (inhabitants)."[1]

Saint Augustine would settle on the Greek *latreia* to describe Christian worship, but for homesteaders, the tension he sensed about the word *cult*, being a word employed both when man looks up to God in worship and down to earth in work, is perfect. Our homesteads and the work involved with them live in this space, unique to man, wherein our prayer and work are two lungs in the same body, physical and spiritual. This is the liturgy of the land.

---

1 Quotes in R. Jared Staudt, *The Primacy of God: The Virtue of Religion in Catholic Theology* (Steubenville, OH: Emmaus Academic, 2022), 35.

CLEAR THINKING

BACK TO THE HOMESTEAD

"Pater meus agricola est" (My Father is a farmer).
—JOHN 15:1[2]

"Go forth, Christian soul, to the unfallen earth, and there amidst the tares and briars sing the song of work that is worship. Soon around your croft will gather a sheaf of homes and homesteads, where the GREAT SACRAMENT may prepare the ploughman for the furrow, the monk for the choir, the priest for the Altar."
—FR. VINCENT MCNABB[3]

The homestead is the natural habitat and setting for home and family. By "setting," we do not merely mean that it is some sort of decoration or "look"; rather, it is a place where the most fundamental work and relationships of man are joined and ordered together for the health of body and soul. Many other arrangements of households and work are good, but the work of a homestead, of tending land with and for a family, is the original design for man's life on earth.

Not only is the homestead secure in what it produces on a practical level (what is more necessary than food?) but it is that place where one works close to those things so

---

2 The translation usually reads that the Father is a "husbandman," as in the Douay-Rheims, or some other specific aspect of farming, but the Vulgate has the word *agricola*, which can be translated simply as "farmer."
3 Vincent McNabb, *The Church and the Land* (Norfolk, VA: IHS Press, 2003), 35.

essential to human flourishing. The homestead experiences and feels the lessons from God through nature, through cooperation with the family, and in the cycles and seasons that represent life itself, like the "resurrection" of spring and the "death" of winter. It is a place where truth is obvious, though that truth is oftentimes as painful and difficult as it is instructive. The homestead is the place where our efforts are directed by and for their true ends, which are the faithful tending of our vocations and the glory of God, our ultimate end.

We have all felt how modern life seems to speed up with a centrifugal-like force that pulls us from the center, the home, each other, and even God. The more we do, the tighter we have to hold on to what matters. The force of it is dizzying and requires much attention and effort to stay close. Sometimes, we feel like we're losing our grip entirely and long for a different way to live, one that draws us back into the center.

We might ask why homesteading, which is also very "busy" and demanding, seems to have a different effect. Instead of pulling us outward, it is a way of life that draws us toward the home and the relationships that matter most. The well-ordered and devout homestead achieves that seemingly impossible goal of bringing the various pulls of life into true balance: work, provision, family, play, nature, and prayer. It does this precisely because it isn't actually bringing anything into balance. Things can only be balanced when they are *separated* for comparison or coordination. Picture a scale with two sides. What we place on the scale is disconnected; that's what makes the comparison of weight possible. The homestead gives a sense of order not because it is balanced but because it *integrates* these things into a working whole by living in the natural setting—the habitat if you will—of the family.

Of all the motivations for moving away from our modern, technologically saturated lives to the simple work of a homestead, one of the best is to reintegrate our lives in a truly human and holy way.

As an example of the difference between integration and balance, just consider spending time with your family. When work is done away from home for most of the day, we often find ourselves trying to cram in quality time in a couple of hours at night and on the weekends. But because our job is at a desk, we might also have to find time for exercise, so we join a gym. And because our children also need exercise, they join a sports team. But because we know that our social life is important too, members of the family join this or that group based on their age, especially for the sake of the mentoring

and formation they need to mature and grow in virtue—at least that should be a reason. And, don't forget, we have to get to Mass and find time for prayer together.

All of these things are good and even necessary. But because they are separate (you can spend hours a day just commuting to activities), we must work hard to keep these different things in balance. Disputes and competition for time disrupt the peace of our family, potentially estranging us from one another, or the less important eclipses the more important. Without proper balance, these competing interests might become something like an autoimmune disease, when the immune system attacks the body it is meant to defend. The good of work, exercise, and even leisure can all jump the bounds of order and, by doing so, attack other goods. Thus, a man may get awards and raises at work but be resented and disrespected at home, even if his paycheck pays the mortgage. A naturally athletic child becomes obsessed with being the best in his sport and finds himself willingly missing Mass to go to a training camp or utterly devastated to the point of despair by an injury. A mother tries to share her wisdom online through a monetized website but gets glued to her phone and grows vain, hypocritical, and artificial.

There are many who are very good at balancing these things and even thrive doing it. It takes a special skill and discipline. Some—perhaps many more—really struggle to keep things together, and as a result, we are seeing a steady disintegration of the family. Without careful balance, good things turn on themselves; things that are meant to live in peace go to war with each other. In fact, one of the most effective attacks of the devil is turning something good into a disordered and self-destructive evil. That is when imbalance becomes disorder, which is an invitation to sin and vice.

By contrast, on the natural homestead, the way of life does indeed draw us back together by *integrating* the good and natural needs of man. The work is right outside, and it involves everyone. And because it is hard work, you can cancel that gym membership; work and exercise are reintegrated. Perhaps the extra food grown there also lowers the grocery bill, allowing you to work fewer hours away from home. This might reintegrate you with your household by simply being present more. Interest in fruit trees, which can be propagated with literally fruitful work and without money, replaces interest in the newest gadget or toy, alleviating further not only the need for more money but the potential vices around wealth. And, in its best form, the work and life of the homestead involve the whole family, so you don't have to squeeze in time together. As often happens, such work draws you into your local community as you look to mentors and neighbors for help and they look to you. This time together and with your community not only fulfills the natural social needs of man and strengthens those relationships but does so in a way that provides opportunities for mentoring and even for fulfilling the plain command to love your neighbors. You can do this in simple and organic ways because you actually know your neighbors and what their true needs are, such as helping with livestock when someone is sick or sharing the abundance of a garden. There is no need to create lessons of responsibility for your children because they actually are responsible for real things. A single activity on the homestead, like butchering a hog with neighbors, can literally bring together a multitude of human needs—from mentoring to exercise to eating—into a single act. As Wendell Berry says in his poem "For the Hog Killing," by the need for food and the communal act of killing and preparing the hog "we renew the bond,"[4] speaking of both the bond to the earth and each other. The work brings together. These things are no longer competing for attention but function together, augmenting and complementing each other. That is integration.

WHY "GO BACK" TO HOMESTEADING?

Here, at the very beginning of this book, we should take a hard look at the most common objection against homesteading: that it is an impractical, romanticized, and unrealistic idea. In short, there's no "going back" because society is just not ordered that way anymore and, what's more, to "go back" is a regression of human progress and genius. "*Back to the land*" is a slogan common to movements with different ideological reasoning—from Catholics to anarchists—but with a common rejection of modern society and a return to a more agrarian (land and farming-based) way of life. After all, one of the most famous books about one of the Catholic "back to the land" movements is called *Flee to the Fields*.[5] Is that what we're doing when we move to a homestead? Running away? Are homesteaders retreating from modern challenges, withdrawing from society, and even failing to fulfill the call of Christians to be lights in a dark world all in search of some selfies with their boutique chickens?

---

4 Wendell Berry, *For the Hog Killing, 1979* (KY: Fireside Industries Books, 2019), 9.
5 Hilaire Belloc and John McQuillan, *Flee to the Fields: The Faith and Works of the Catholic Land Movement* (Norfolk: HIS Press 2003).

Instead of "going back" to some agrarian idealism, some might argue, it would be better to make peace with our improved lives and show a little more gratitude for all our material abundance and speedy connectivity. If it is the case that modern man not only moved away from the farm naturally but "escaped" its drudgery, it is not without reason that we might ask, Why go "back" to something that our ancestors left behind?

There are two simple answers to the charge of "going backward" against progress. The first is that the very idea of progress that undergirds the charge comes from post-enlightenment and secularist philosophies that essentially see modern man as the best form of humanity *because it is the latest*. It is a theory not unlike, and not unrelated, to evolutionary theory that considers the "most evolved" form to be the best simply because it out-survived weaker creatures that were ill-suited to the challenges of real life. In other words, version 3.0 of a system is always better than version 2.0, and certainly better than 1.0. But that is precisely what must be challenged, that the latest version is the best version. Clearly, from a spiritual and even natural perspective, we are not only free to question the outcomes of all of our "progress," but in the face of the breakdown of the family, of local communities, and of religious belief, we are forced to ask harder questions about the directions we have been going. Often, those that want to homestead are rethinking not just where food comes from but the foundations on which our lives are really built.

The second answer to the "going backward" charge is related to the first, but instead of thinking in terms of a timeline (*this* point in history is better than *that* point in history, so we should imitate that), it is a charge that homesteading is merely another lifestyle made possible by the modern order. Perhaps wannabe homesteaders are choosing to imitate some ideal in their imagination, thus demonstrating that they are merely finding another way to enjoy the modern life made possible by technology and the global economy. In that sense, homesteading is not unlike all of the other lifestyle choices of modern man. We might even see the various homesteading movements that come and go as nothing more than other lifestyle fads that only a wealthy and spoiled society could embrace. Perhaps this charge carries more water than the other, but the simple response is that homesteading is not just another lifestyle among others but a primordial one; it is something in us that needs to work with land and family under God's care. Even if one is homesteading simply because one can afford to, like a wealthy and retired couple, perhaps it is still good to do so. The act and art of cultivating the land can be pursued on a very large spectrum of engagement and true *need*, but that it gets done and becomes more foundational for life and culture is still something good and necessary, as we will see throughout this book.

Our goal as homesteaders and with this book is not merely to recreate some point in time. We're not just buying period clothing and a butter churn to look a certain way on social media. We are also not merely rejecting everything modern and accepting anything old. Man lives from the earth; it is a reality ever ancient and new. What we are trying to do is live in accord with our created nature while accepting and responding to the realities around us. What we are going "back" to is the philosophical principle that the homestead is the first and most natural place for the family, and that is the reason that it is a place of human flourishing and happiness. "[God] gave man the earth for his cultivation," said Pope Pius XII, "as the most beautiful and honorable occupation in the natural order."[6] The homestead, in other words, is a gift from God and not a construct of man. Pope Pius XII also said that our modern industrialized society and the natural agrarian society "produces altogether different men."[7] We are not only free to ask if we can build our lives on different foundations, producing "altogether different men," but compelled to.

NOT ORGANIC

Another important consideration when we speak of society "leaving" the homestead is that the process—the loss of agrarian economies and households—was not organic. The reason most of us are no longer farmers is because society was rearranged by man in that way.

Catholic historian and scholar Alan C. Carlson helps show that families, especially in the United States, did not "leave" the land at all but have been moved from it by policy and practice. If it is something artificially imposed on the family, especially if it has had a traceably negative effect, then there are stronger arguments to push back and do our best to "go back." Carlson's work has shown that suburban developments have been an intentional objective of government housing policy for close to a century, and these

---

6 Pius XII, *The Life of a Farmer,* from *The Major Addresses of Pope Pius XII*, vol. 1 (St. Paul, MN: The North Central Publishing Company, 1961), 98.

7 Pius XII, 99.

policies had explicit goals to increase urban populations with the obvious and intentional side effect of depleting the countryside of its farmers. The "suburban experiment," as Carlson calls it, refers to homes being built in a fashion foreseeing that they would not be places of production but of *consumption*. The more money moves the better.

As an example of these policies that preferred suburbanization, we can consider that almost all homes in the United States once housed spaces for work, food preparation and storage (like cellars), and often even room enough for multiple generations. But in the middle and later 1900s, official policies put us on a different course. For example, mortgage guidelines from the FHA "were systematically denied to any residence that contained facilities designed for use as a productive shop, office, or separate apartment for an extended family member or renter, or preschool," explains Carlson.[8] The government *wanted* to phase out rural and productive homes in favor of consolidated suburban neighborhoods as a necessary part of a consumer-based, industrial economy.

There is a logic to the government preferring non-productive, suburban homes. Productive homes, like homesteads, remove people from the workforce, reduce the need to purchase new products (consume industrially manufactured goods), and do not generate taxable income nor contribute to the revenue from various sales taxes.

The encouragement of suburbanization also coincided with policies in agriculture often summarized as "get big or get out," which refers to the consolidation of farms into larger and larger ones, the obvious side effect being fewer farms, which means less farmers. Many can speak well of the low price of food, but the cost has been the loss of farming as a way of life, a general reduction of crop diversity, and lower nutrient density in food (i.e., less healthy food). Wendell Berry has famously traced the policies and their effects in books like *The Unsettling of America*, which points out that America was "settled" by farmers but then the farmers were systematically extinguished, "unsettled," over time in favor of a corporate and industrialized model. What Berry and many others have shown is that the cost of cheap food is much higher than we have acknowledged.

---

8 Allan Carlson, *From Cottage to Work Station* (San Francisco: Ignatius Press, 1993), 76.

When we think of a farmhouse, we often think of a small, even impoverished dwelling. But traditional societies often built large homes because it was more economical to house multiple generations, as well as workspace, in the same structure. Pictured here is the farmhouse where St. John Bosco was born, which housed many family members.

Large corporations and investors have also been happy and eager to see farmers leave the land. In the last century, as the number of farmers decreased, the size of farms increased. This was possible because of modern machinery, but it also happened because farming went from the common work of the common man to big business. A family owning a small farm could never be said to be an image of material wealth (i.e., rich with cash), but corporations owning the productive power of hundreds or thousands of those of farms could turn a real and consistent profit, and the need for the product will never go away since people don't just want it but need it three times a day. That's just good business. Therefore, as families left the farms behind, not only did large corporations and speculators gain their labor in the factories in the city, but they gained the land those workers left behind too.

We should note that farming on a large scale does not necessarily mean more food per acre. A man with a spade and a hoe can grow significantly more per acre than a massive farm plowed with a tractor because, as the unofficial chaplain of England's "Catholic Land Movement" Fr. Vincent McNabb point out, "whereas [machines] produces less

per acre, it deceives men because it can deal with more acres."[9] If we are considering farming *first* as a way of life that also produces food for society, then this is not a net gain. If we think only in terms of production, forgetting culture and tradition, then the loss might not even register.

The housing policy of the government not only moved slowly away from the productive home, especially the farm, but even stopped being based on the family in general. For example, the original 1949 Housing Act explicitly purposed to create homes for families, but in 1982, the word "family" was dropped altogether, showing that the practice and policy of the country had "evolved" to be about houses, not households.[10] Remember, an unhealthy family is not necessarily bad for the economy. More houses based on making and spending money are better than productive, self-sufficient, and intergenerational households.

A family that moves from a homestead to an urban center becomes, by necessity, a more prolific earner so that it can be a consistent consumer and taxable base. If that same home splits into two homes through a divorce, then the consuming power of a home is doubled (two Christmases, two mortgages, more cars, more gas, and so on). And such breakdowns have become significantly more common and possible in the

---

9 Vincent McNabb, *Old Principles and the New Order* (Providence, RI: Cluny), 100.
10 Carlson, *From Cottage to Work Station*, 84.

modern economy. Something has gone wrong. One of the reasons the sexual revolution has been so devastating to the family is that the foundation for disintegration was laid when the family became only a consuming unit. The procreative end of the family still gave it a clear purpose. But when the inherent consumerism was applied to sexuality—sex as an individual's desires pursued for the individual's fulfillment—the final strand holding it all together seemed to break. Our housing policy and our sexual revolution coincided in disastrous ways. "America's massive program had turned on itself," Carlson says of this general policy, "consuming the very social units it was intended to serve; yet few seemed to notice, even fewer seemed to care."[11]

THE EFFECT

What happens when the family no longer works together in the shared economy of the home itself? The observable state of the family is that it is in decline, but many focus only on decayed morals and the negative impact of secularization. While these factors matter, it is also clear that the family has a hard time with cohesion and relevance when it only lives together.

Social commentator Robert Nisbet has interpreted and articulated the trend well, pointing out that when a home loses its functionality—its practical usefulness and productivity—it becomes a place primarily for emotional support. Lacking shared work and a practical mutual dependence, the primary purpose of the family is to give unquestioning support to the individual's interests, success, and endeavors. But being "supportive" meant something very different in times past. It meant that individuals support the family, not vice versa. "In earlier ages," says Nisbet, "kinship was inextricably involved in the process of getting a living, providing education, supporting the infirm, caring for the aged, and maintaining religious values. In vast rural areas, until quite recently, the family was the actual agency of economic production, distribution, and consumption."[12] In our present time, it is clear that the family "has progressed from institution to companionship" precisely because it doesn't do anything productive together.[13]

Without the functional dynamic, it becomes more difficult to instill the truth that the family is the "basis of society," as we often tell ourselves and our children. This is

---

11 Carlson, 84.
12 Robert Nisbet, *The Quest for Community* (Wilmington, DE: ISI Books, 2014), 52.
13 Nisbet, 53.

simply because as soon as they walk out the door of the home, they see and sense that the family is *not* the basis of our society in its actual functioning, and this is related directly to the fact that the family is not the meaningful center or even purpose of much of our work and economic reality.

THE ERODED SOIL OF FAITH

There is another side effect when the family loses its cultural significance and cohesion: the loss of faith. The secular world likes to credit itself for "defeating" faith, claiming that advancement in science and technology has simply displaced the unreasonable and superstitious need for religion. However, Catholic sociologist Mary Eberstadt[14] has shown how it is the very ordering of society away from the family, away from home, that has had the greatest impact on religious practice. Clearly, we have "lost God" in the West, but she shows that it happened alongside the process of industrialization, which had the side effect of disrupting family cohesion, much more than the attacks from atheists. When individuals are raised without meaningful and practical bonds of home, something made possible by industrialization, technology, mobility, and specialization especially, they tend to drift into the dangerous waters of the world much more easily. Men, for example, are significantly more likely to continue in their faith when they have work to share with their children, and children are much more likely to continue in faith if it is reinforced by the presence and example of the father's work.[15]

In other words, the Church is losing members not because she is losing the argument but because she is losing the family. Removing work from the home has removed people from the home. This movement made the bonds of family more strained, and when the stretched threads snap, people fall away from each other and God. That fall, if you will, is in the same direction and with the same momentum.

Eberstadt also reminds us of the connection between apostasy and the increase of mammon made possible by the increased material production of today's working world. The reordering of society through industrialization and suburbanization is founded upon material abundance; it's a defining characteristic. While on the one hand, we can

---

14 I am relying on Mary Eberstadt, *How the West Really Lost God: A New Theory of Secularization* (West Conshohocken, PA: Templeton Press).

15 These points are well documented in Eberstadt's book, as well as Dr. Paul Vitz's book *The Faith of the Fatherless* (San Francisco: Ignatius Press, 2013).

be amazed at the sheer volume and security of material goods, we do well to consider the effect of wealth on the soul. "What caused secularization?" asks Eberstadt. "Material progress did. People got fat and happy and didn't need God anymore."[16] Eberstadt points out that this should not be surprising. Our Lord lays out the choice, telling us we cannot serve God and mammon (see Mt 6:24; Lk 16:13).

In summary, what Carlson and others have shown is that the move away from an agrarian society was not an organic market development but a *move*—a construct of man—specifically from government policy and the large corporations investing in farm production for profit. Today, the largest farmland owner in the United States is Bill Gates,[17] second only to the United States government itself. And the policy worked: in the 1800s, nearly 90 percent of Americans were farmers. Today, less than 1 percent are farmers. And the family can live happily in the new arrangement, but not without great effort. We are reasonable, therefore, to seek a different model. We could put it this way:

---

16 Eberstadt, *How the West Really Lost God,* 81. Carlson, *From Cottage to Work Station,* 76.

17 Ariel Shapiro, "America's Biggest Owner Of Farmland Is Now Bill Gates," *Forbes,* January 14, 2021, https ://www.forbes.com/sites/arielshapiro/2021/01/14/americas-biggest-owner-of-farmland-is-now-bill-gates -bezos-turner/?sh=539edaef6096.

the displacement of man from his God-given occupation of farmer required the construct of a man-made alternative in the modern economic order. What we homesteaders want is to receive back a gift from God that was taken away by man. We would be delusional to think that starting a homestead would be a magic fix to all of our problems. We would be even more delusional, however, to think that it isn't a very important and reasonable step for many toward living a more natural and family-friendly life.

WHO THIS BOOK IS FOR

We have written this book based on our experience that confirms the truth of the homesteading family. Both of us "converted" to a life of homesteading and farming around the same time, and we have been comparing notes the whole time, making many mistakes but also finding the truth that the homestead is a beautiful and holy place for a family. We do get to work alongside our family. We have delighted in the fruits of the earth and our labor. We have been able to slow down and enjoy the unique communication of God's life that comes with being in nature more.

But we have also experienced the tension and difficulty of converting to a way of life at odds with much of society's logic and rhythms. We have not fully integrated our whole life, and we recognize that the tension between the modern world and the harmonious homestead does not resolve overnight, so we still have to find a balance between office jobs, part-time jobs, and the demands of a farm. We did not inherit farming as a tradition, meaning we had the challenge of learning it as an art we are not trained in (despite what you might see online, learning to homestead will not come from watching videos). It has been humbling and trying. We have, therefore, written the book that would have been helpful to us in those early years, those that want to go from *here* to *there* on a homestead.

Classicist and Catholic professor John Senior said that it is much easier to make a college boy from a farmer than a farmer from a college boy. The practical, economic, and even emotional challenges are massive. We use the word "conversion" to homesteading intentionally because the more one goes toward the land for life and sustenance, the more you realize how different it is from modern, secular, and consumerist living. It works on a completely different logic, and the more you order your life around the homestead, the more things of modern life you might necessarily leave behind.

Some people will have economic and practical realities that might make the challenge seem insurmountable. We have included, therefore, a large section on some practical considerations for ordering your family differently even if you have to stay put in your current setting that is presumably *not* within an agrarian context.

We should be careful of a prideful and flippant proclamation of "going back to the land," as if anyone could do it and the skills of farmers are nothing but "hacks" to getting food out of dirt. Homesteading is not another occupation or hobby that is simply a matter of technical application of facts. Where will you go? Who will teach you? What about money and mortgages and retirement? These are questions worth asking and answering if one is serious about investing a considerable amount of time, capital, and effort into the endeavor, especially when many have noted that novice homesteaders throw in the towel after only two to three years—long before the fruit of their labor can even be appreciated. What if you upend a life and family only to find yourself forced back to a "normal" life? In other words, we want to be careful that the trend to homesteading isn't that, a trend or fad destined to disappoint.[18]

Understanding and examining our motivation for homesteading, therefore, is a helpful step in considering it as a way of life. This book's contribution to that consideration is not in the technical aspects of growing and harvesting, though we will touch on that regarding broad decision-making. There are already many great resources on the practicality of working the land. What we want to do is point out that this *life of integration*—of work, land, family, leisure, and home—should be approached with a truly Catholic lens. This helps not only in defining success on the homestead but in finding true human happiness. To do that, we must understand that the work of the homesteader, the liturgy of the land, requires a recalibration of both thought and action. The Catholic homestead is simply built on different foundations than those of today's secular world, and we must understand those foundations, aided by faith, for the house to be built to last. "Unless the Lord builds the house," says the psalmist, "those who build it labor in vain" (Ps 127:1).

---

18 For some observations of those that come and go to the land, see Amanda Fuhriman, "Homesteading is trending but don't be fooled: 'You work 10 times more when you live this life,'" Remote Family, March 7, 2023, https://www.remotefamily.com/homesteading-trend/.

CHAPTER

— 2 —

FROM DIVISION OF LABOR TO INTEGRATED WORK

"In the ordinary daily life of men in Christian culture, who work not only in the sweat of their brows, but for love of their families, there is also a love of work. When men cut wood or go to war or make love to their wives, and when women spin or wash and reciprocate that love, they are working not only to get the job done so that children will be born and grow and have clothes to wear and food to eat. They are working so that one day those children will be saints in heaven."

—JOHN SENIOR[19]

From the very beginning of creation, man is called to work. The work that man begins in Eden at the command of God is not simply an activity like the beasts of the earth, but it constitutes man's very nature, his relationship with the world and with God. In relationship with nature, man brings forth goods from the earth that are gifts from God that arrive through his work. Our work, therefore, is both activity and receptivity, effort and gift, something we work for and inherit at the same time. In relation to God, man's work is an extension, a continuation, of God's creative act as the Father. To work with nature, therefore, is to work as a child of God, and this sense of identity shapes how we

---

19 John Senior, *The Death of Christian Culture* (Norfolk, VA: IHS Press, 2008), 26.

see our work. Through our work, we are who we are as the "lords" of the earth in right relationship with the Lord of all, as John Paul II said:

> Man is made to be in the visible universe an image and likeness of God himself, and he is placed in it in order to subdue the earth. From the beginning therefore he is called to work. Work is one of the characteristics that distinguish man from the rest of creatures, whose activity for sustaining their lives cannot be called work. Only man is capable of work, and only man works, at the same time by work occupying his existence on earth. Thus work bears a particular mark of man and of humanity, the mark of a person operating within a community of persons. And this mark decides its interior characteristics; in a sense it constitutes its very nature.[20]

God is ever at work. "My Father is working still," said Jesus, "and I am working" (Jn 5:17). When Mary and Joseph find Jesus in the temple as a young man, He is about His Father's business. God is not *like us* in that He is at work, but we are *like Him* when we work as His sons like His Son.

Homesteading is principally a matter of work. When one separates, for example, from the provided comforts of modern life by the use of something like a woodstove instead of a thermostat, he is *increasing* his work. Clearly, one of the principal differences between an industrialized society and that of the homestead is expressed in this very point: what work is, why we do it, and what the effect of work is on the soul.

INDUSTRIAL DIVISION

In the last few centuries, industrialization was a change not merely in technique but also in the very idea and anthropology of man. Specifically, God was forced out of the public sphere of economics and politics, and man was reconceived as something other than a son of God. Neil Postman has noted that the shift in the population from productive families to consuming houses comes from an admixture of confidence in technology, unapologetic consumerism, and an anthropological and even theological shift in what we understand man and his communities to be. Though not a Catholic, he sees the

---

20 John Paul II, Encyclical *Laborem Exercens* (September 14, 1981).

theological problem that redefines what a man is: "We had learned how to invent things, and the question of why we invent things receded in importance. The idea that if something could be done it should be done was born in the nineteenth century. And along with it, there developed a profound belief in all the principles through which invention succeeds: objectivity, efficiency, expertise, standardization, measurement, and progress. It also came to be believed that the engine of technological progress worked most efficiently when people are conceived of not as children of God or even as citizens but as consumers—that is to say, markets."[21]

He accurately uses the word "belief" to describe this tendency because there is an observable, even religious dedication of some to a particular ideal of progress that does indeed reduce households and communities to little more than markets. Postman is right: to live conscious of being God's children changes how we live, including work and providing for our true needs.

The industrialization of society is made possible by, in a sense, breaking up the "whole" units of productive homes and even communities so that the laborers can be divided into repetitive and mundane jobs on the lower end and specialized jobs of expertise on the other. In doing so, the economy of scale and material abundance is undeniable, but it has brought about a near-constant tension in the understanding and practice of work in relationship to family life. The Church's concern has been consistent: instead of work being done by man for true and good ends, industrial work uses man for profit—as a means to an end. As Pope Pius XII famously described more base practices of industrialization, "And thus bodily labor, which Divine Providence decreed to be performed, even after original sin, for the good at once of man's body and soul, is being everywhere changed into an instrument of perversion; for dead matter comes forth from the factory ennobled, while men there are corrupted and degraded."[22]

The division of jobs and the ordering of them for the sake of production is to treat labor and work—and the people that do the work—as an essentially mechanical thing, a machine. (This is perhaps why we have so unapologetically allowed machines to replace man in factories today because that was what man already was to the factory model.) But man is not a machine. Nature is not a machine. The most inconvenient things to

---

21   Neil Postman, *Technopoly: The Surrender of Culture to Technology* (New York: Vintage Books, 1993), 42.
22   Pius XII, Encyclical *Quadragesimo Anno* (May 15, 1931), no. 135.

efficiency and dependability (i.e., unchanging and unchangeable) are these very things, nature and humans. It seems that the underlying foundations of modern industrialism and our love for technological advancement did not stop at making laborious jobs easier with machines, but by conquering nature totally, without the limits of nature, we failed to limit the technological domination of ourselves. With the advent of artificial intelligence, we are now eager to even let machines *think* for us. In many ways, by homesteading, we are taking work back from the machines so that we can enjoy it once again as God intended. The reason industrialism tends to be so dehumanizing and violent toward nature is that it stands as something wholly different. Industrialism has given us much, but in order to control the uncontrollable, it has required the disintegration of man working from and with nature directly. It is wrong to characterize homesteading as simply being "anti" technology; rather, this view deals with the nature and value of working directly with the things God has given us, the raw materials and simple relationships that are truly the stuff of life.

This is at the heart of the liturgy of the land. Liturgy, after all, means the work of the people. Fundamentally, the liturgy of the land reintegrates peoples into each other and into the land *through work*.

DIFFERENT MOTIVATIONS

In our experience and study, it seems that men and women come to desire homesteading for different reasons, and appreciating these differences makes possible the integration of that work back at home. Mothers and fathers are accustomed to their work straining them apart, demanding their division. Rarely is work a place of union at all, a place of relationship. Yet, the difference between the sexes is joined together in complementarity on the homestead, instead of the competitive nature in the world's economic understanding. Considering how men and women are different, and how they are united most beautifully in the work of the home, can help tremendously as new homesteaders learn to live the liturgy of the land as a family.

To consider these differences, we can turn to God's curses given to man after the Fall. It is an interesting but often missed detail of God's address to the newly sinful man that He addresses Adam and Eve separately. And, notably, He addresses the reality of their relationship to work and each other.

THE FATHER'S BUSINESS

When God addresses Adam, we learn that his work of "subduing the earth" continues, but it is going to get harder. His relationship with nature has changed because nature has sensed and responded to the rebellion of sin. But in relation to the family unit, Adam's work is oriented outward to the procuring of practical needs for his family. This outward orientation, as many men know, can be a place of great tension. Man can go out to the field to provide for his family and not return. Not only can our hands go outward toward work, away from home, but our hearts can too, and this can be exacerbated when the challenge of work loses its grounding in the purpose of the family, which starts in providing for their bodily needs but encompasses their whole humanity as well, body and soul. The drift of men away from their homes often starts at work. Or, similarly but through a different pull, man's work—the thorns and thistles of it all—simply take him away from his family by force, taking the best of him and leaving little else for the family.

Therefore, many fathers find themselves desiring to work (and work harder!) on the homestead as a primary means of connecting with their families. In suburbanization and industrialization, work is separated from the home to the extent that neighbors and even family members can live alongside each other without even knowing what each other does for a living. This does not instill appreciation and respect as easily as work done in sight of and with each other. The home becomes a place of mutual support and love, but not practical support and help as it does with homesteading. This environment is particularly difficult for a father because men are the heads of the home but are not always the best at intuiting all of the emotional and "softer" needs of the human heart and are much more attuned, in his outward orientation, to the practical needs, the "harder" needs of food and shelter. But as a farm benefits from the presence of the farmer ("a farmer's feet are the best fertilizer," is an old saying), so too the father gains a better understanding of the human needs of his family as he is close by, not just having them reported to him later by his wife or teachers.

Therefore, fathers desire to bring their outward work right outside the door by working together, with their family, and leading the home as an enterprise as much as a place of sleeping and eating. Men are much better at creating opportunities for human connection through shared work and responsibility than they are at trying to orchestrate and conduct emotional connection without this context. In other words, men connect beautifully and naturally with those they love through the self-gift of love

manifested in and alongside work. They are less apt to lead in a way that is perceptively masculine—fatherly—if all of their interactions are more like a counseling session done away from "real life." Men are able to lead as fathers when the home is, in a sense, a business and not just a place to eat and talk and watch amusements with others. This should not be construed to be some machismo reduction of masculinity to practical activity, but there is a natural intertwining of hearts through shared work, as Our Lord says He is continuing the work of the Father and, therefore, must be about the Father's business.

Working with, for, and alongside his family also frees a man from seeing himself as the sole bread winner of a family, as if the nature of bread is that it must be won. As we know from the Our Father, "bread" is a gift from the Father through the father, a gift more than a prize. The idea of the father as the primary monetary earner has some historic precedence, but broadly speaking, the family as a whole is engaged in true and actual work; they are not just consumers of the father's income as the Marxists famously saw the natural familial arrangement.[23] Pope Pius XII noted as much about

---

23 Fredrick Engels famously called the wife and children of a home the "proletariat" of the house, with the father as a sort of tyrant controlling them by holding all of the true wealth.

farmers and craftsmen: "That the rest of the family should also contribute to the common support [with the father], according to the capacity of each, is certainly right, as can be observed especially in the families of farmers, but also in the families of many craftsmen and small shopkeepers."[24]

THE MOTHER'S CARE AND CULTURE

Now we can turn to women on the homestead through the lens of Eve. When God addresses Eve after the Fall, we hear two things. In the first place, we learn that her essential and higher work of maternity will, like Adam's primary work, be harder than before. She will continue the work of mothering but with its own thorns and thistles of pain and difficulty. By sin, not only does the body of nature rebel against us, but our own bodies do as well. The other detail is that she will now have desire for Adam, which refers to a desire to have control over the hierarchy of the home of which the father is the head, but God says she will still be subject to him as the head of the home. These might seem like two very different things and even arbitrary, but what we see is a fundamental disruption in the way that a woman relates within her household.

Although femininity is often reduced to just receptivity, in many classical and theological senses, femininity refers to a sort of wholeness, a "body" if you will. That which goes out from the body becomes masculine by its separation from the body but still being *for* the body, and this is male. A priest, for example, is male and comes forth from the Church, who is a she, for the sake of that Church. The Church, as a woman, a bride, gathers in the Church into the wholeness of it as a family; picture the arms of St. Peter's square reaching out to draw in and encompass all man into the family of God. Other examples might be how we use the feminine "she" to refer to a ship on the sea, encompassing individual passengers. We might call an individual country a fatherland, but we call the earth as a whole a mother. Wisdom itself, which is not just the knowledge of individual facts but a form of knowing that is intuitive and whole, is called in Greek by the name *Sophia*. The only time Our Lord refers to Himself in the feminine is when He is looking out over Jerusalem and imagines being a mother hen that gathers in the scattered chicks.

Therefore, it makes sense that the bodily sense of Eve is somewhat disrupted by the Fall. Childbirth, the care and bodily sustaining of life itself, is Eve's beautiful gift to the

---

24 Pius XII, Encyclical *Quadragesimo Anno* (May 15, 1931), no. 71.

world, but it becomes more challenging. This is also revealing when we think of many women finding their desire for homesteading not just in having their husband closer to home but in the concern of having healthy food for the body and bodies of the family. Whereas men often think of the work of food in its outwardness, women tend to think of the nutritive quality of the food for her family, and this desire for more natural and healthy food drives her to homestead for the health benefits of the work, the inward and bodiliness of it if you will.

This has a relationship to her subjection to Adam, which is disrupted by a new desire that comes after the Fall. The word used there is the same one used when God tells Cain, just before he kills Abel, that sin is crouching at his door and its desire is for him. The desire of Eve is related to a desire to dominate, to control. As the head, the father must lead and provide. As the body, Eve is in a relationship of submission, yes, but if we think of it in a bodily form and not a worldly or Marxist vying for power and the control of resources, we see a harmony and wholeness that is beautiful in its *compatibility*. Women are much better at intuiting and sensing the broader "softer" needs of the whole family, which are not restricted to emotional health. Women, for example, often intuit a sickness of physical disruption better than a man. In a strong marriage, the wife will take her insights of the needs of the body to the head, who receives them with love and attention and acts on them. We might consider the marriage of Christ with the Church, of the Head in heaven listening closely to the needs of the Church as expressed in prayer.

We should note that the other way we know this bodily understanding of the family, and the relationship of men and women, is not merely a matter of power and authority but is in the analogy to our actual bodies and heads. If the man is the head of the family as represented by the use of the intellect, and the female represents the sensitivity of the body, we should remember that Saint Thomas Aquinas teaches us that "man cannot use his reason without his sensitive powers, man needs to sustain his body in order that he may use his reason."[25] A man cannot exercise his headship without the body of the family, his wife. Some men erroneously try to assert their headship in ways learned in the world and at work, which is often in hierarchies and orders, which are good, but they are not *hierarchical bodies*. The headship of a body, especially when we keep in mind Jesus Christ, is something wholly different from the job of a manager, general, or boss.

---

25 *Summa Theologica*, II-II, q. 142, art. 1, ad. 2.

In other words, a man cannot bring a woman into objectified submission, but he must love and care for her because he *needs* her to be what she is as much as she needs him. A severed head is dead. Similarly, the sensitivity of a woman is offered lovingly to her husband and, like the Church in her prayers to the Head, she is confident in and receptive to his love and leadership.

INTEGRATION OF THE SEXES

Obviously, these differences are the points of tension in much of modern society, but on the homestead, the shared work of the household brings these things into integration. On the one hand, the wife often *sees plainly* the work of the father and holds and presents a great respect for that work. The father offers himself as a gift by bringing the goods of his labor to her. Close by, she informs and appeals to him on behalf of the family's needs, and he hears and directs his work toward the body of the family and his own wife.

In opposition to the world's attempt at bringing men and women together by diminishing or denying their differences, because the differences are disrupted by the control necessary in modern production, the difference between men and women is *highlighted* on the homestead. This differentiation should and does engender a greater harmony as it brings the shared work—the outwardness and inwardness of men and women—into a proper relationship. A symphony is beautiful because of fifty different instruments playing in harmony, not fifty of the same instrument doing the same thing equally. Whereas the world uses the logic of machines and powerbrokers to reduce men and women into coexisting relationships—often by either trying to make women more manly or men more womanly—the Church teaches that it is only in the family that the union is in its natural, integrated, and fruitful form—the codependence of true peace. Pope Pius XI pointed out that the "Creator has ordained and disposed perfect union of the sexes only in matrimony."[26] As we have argued throughout, the context of matrimony, of the family, does not exclude work, but this does show us that because the homestead is the natural setting of the family, the shared work of the home brings about this perfect union. As Aristotle put it, "There is no greater blessing on earth than when husband and wife rule their home in harmony of mind and will."[27]

We should also note that the homestead alleviates the strain people feel between the so-called traditional wife and husband of the last century and the modern working mother and father today. Some extol movements to recover the image of the 1950s, for example, but forget that the dividing of the home from work—sending dad off and keeping mom home to keep things tidy and cook—is not the natural order of the home. The 1950s were not the height of traditional society that was undone by the craziness of the '60s and '70s, but it was the time when the strain on family cohesion reached the point of snapping, spilling an inner disorder outward in the following decades. It isn't a matter of who stays home and who works but why the home should have its own work. For example, Sacred Scripture praises the wife who goes out and buys fields to have them planted (see Prv 31). That is certainly an economic activity, and one much more ancient than the "tradition" of the early 1900s. Those arguing between the stay-at-home mother and the working mother fail to see that this tension only arises when work has nothing to do with home, or if we reduce all work to the workforce and its making and churning of money. The homestead might grow crops and babies all without the direct use of money, and both of those activities are truly work, even if there's no paycheck. K. L. Kenrick, a schoolmaster that worked with the distributist movement in England

---

26   Pius XI, Encyclical *Divini Illius Magistri* (December 31, 1929), no. 68.
27   Aristotle, *Economics*, Book 3, Section 4.

associated with G. K. Chesterton, noted well the tension when a mother and father grow in an unnatural relationship through the loss of the homestead:

> The wife and mother of today feels that she is a mere parasite upon the husband and father, as indeed she is, because she makes no real contribution to the economic life of the family. Nearly everything needed in the home is made in the factory and bought from the shop already for immediate use and consumption. An Irishman might say that the "mutual dependence" of husband and wife is all on one side. The impact of this conviction on many women is such as to make them feel either that they are a mere toy or else an intolerable burden. Hence the demand for "economic independence," and the eagerness of women to enter the labour market, and to drive men out of employment by working for lower wages. The use of machinery in so many occupations makes the superior strength of men of no advantage in his competition with women. More frequently it is a direct handicap.[28]

The compelling reason for a mother to stay at home on the homestead is not because she doesn't have real economic work to do but because she does. Work is something in human nature for both men and women. The home isn't filled with a mother's presence because that's "where she belongs" but because that is where she naturally works. As we've been arguing, the same is true for the father. Everyone belongs in the home, and work is a common task for all. That the wife followed her husband into the workforce to contribute to the home is logical and not against the traditional family. Her economic independence is not a longing to be unbound from her husband but to join him at work. That the two end up disintegrating from each other is a logical outcome of the economic arrangement, not a violation of roles. In other words, homesteading helps us recover the natural family, not just an ironically iconic image of one.

That the "liberation" of women means, essentially, leaving the home with its duties and responsibilities is a terrible assault on the natural order of family life. It seems that the home can only be conceived of as a prison when it loses function and, therefore,

---

28 K. L. Kenrick, *Flee to the Fields: The Faith and Works of the Catholic Land Movement* (Norfolk, VA: HIS Press, 2003), 114.

meaning. Other disorderly views of the home—from a place of amusement, boredom, and so on—are similar disorders from a loss of purpose. That the wife is "bound" to the home is no different from the husband. The very word *husband* comes from the words *house-bound*.

When we have conducted homesteading workshops for men and women, it is always interesting how the men tend toward very functional, even challenging workshops like how to castrate pigs, whereas the women tend toward what we could call the cultural workshops of receiving raw materials from the land and culturing them into meals and craft, like butter and candle-making, for example. This is that bodily aspect of femininity that takes in the goods of the land and creates a human culture with it. How different this is from the industrial model, which takes in the goods of the land and creates products for consumption and, therefore, a loss of a home-based culture.

It is an undeniable fact of nature that a man is more apt, through his greater upper body strength, to process and split firewood. It is a beautiful reality of womanhood that her care for the home is what actually elevates the work of man into true culture, especially through meals and the ceremonial around them. His work is outward but not absolutely, as he comes and goes within the home. Her work is inward, but her care in the garden and henhouse, for example, brings her into integrated contact with the whole place.

MATURITY AND COMPETENCY

The work of the homestead, shared between men and women, becomes work that is shared with fathers and mothers. In fact, it is uniquely true on the homestead that the integration of children becomes more possible and fruitful. We must admit that without the work of production, members of a family are more akin to consumers of the primary source of income and not an economic value, so to speak. When children are not oriented toward maturing in mind and body so as to help on the farm or in the workshop, we can more easily see them merely as a mouth to feed and not a hand to the plow. Our society today typically pays for all of the expenses of children, only to send them off in their working years to their separate lives. The reason children were so treasured in traditional agrarian societies was not merely that they were treasured as family and kin but also that they added to the economic power of the family. Although this could be disordered or utilitarian just as anything human, it is also the created

nature of man that we benefit from the intergenerational work of a household. Even if it were possible to forget the life our parents gave us, it is even enshrined in the Ten Commandments to honor our parents, which, in Scripture, we know means more than just phone calls and has to do with practical care and providing and living.

HOW CHILDREN BECOME ADULTS

One of the greatest gifts of the homestead is that it can be a place of initiation into manhood and womanhood. Unlike plants and animals, men can be said to have two parts of maturity, one related to the body and the other related to the soul. Unlike animals, our maturity does not stop or terminate in sexual fecundity. Once we reach physical maturity, it is time to grow in character and practice into men and women. Here there is an intertwining in man between his physical maturity and his spiritual, or immaterial, maturity in the form of virtue and belonging. Saint Paul famously said that when he was a boy, he acted like one, but when he became a man he "gave up childish ways" (1 Cor 13:11–12). The Church recognizes that spiritual maturity is a mirror of natural maturity. "[As] nature intends that all her children should grow up and attain full maturity," as the Council of Trent said speaking of natural creatures like plants and animals, "so the Catholic Church, the common mother of all, earnestly desires . . . the perfection of manhood be completed."[29] Similarly, learning to use spiritual gifts is but a mirror of learning to use natural strengths. Saint Paul says to the Ephesians that their gifts are there precisely so that through the work done by them, the souls would grow "to mature manhood" (see Eph 4). The use of physical strength, intellectual attention, and the skill in working within the created world—including with others—is a form of initiation into maturity for boys and girls—that through work and mentoring they would become men and women.

In traditional societies, people matured their children by integrating them into the culture of men and women. This was in essence an enculturation into the work of that place and people. Therefore, although there ought to be plenty of time for play and rest, as a child grew to his strength, the use and purpose of that strength were directed toward its natural end: sharing the work of the homestead for the provision of the household. At a very young age, therefore, the work of the home was the predominating activity of

---

29 Pius V, *The Catechism of Council of Trent* (TAN Books), 219–20.

the household, shaping how it ordered itself. This means that, quite naturally, the maturity of the children was brought about by actual responsibility, the honing of skill and knowledge, and the relational integration with adults and their work.

Boys, for example, would naturally long to join the men in their work, leaving the direct care of the mothers behind. By literally separating from that world, the apron strings get cut and a boy learns the ways of men, by and with men. Young women, for whom maturity comes more naturally but not without formation, learn the gift that they bear within their femininity by growing in the likeness of the mother in her care for the body of the home.

Homes today are predominated by two outside forces that do not naturally orient us toward maturity. On the one hand is the work of the parents, which rarely, if ever, has any need or use for the presence of children. Children are left at home or with others so that parents can go to work. On the other hand are the activities of the children in the various groups, activities, and sports they are involved with. These activities require the money and time of adults, and parents offer this to their children lovingly so that the primary shared activity of the whole household is oriented toward the work of children. When parents aren't working, they're navigating the calendars of the family based on what the kids are doing. Therefore, the maturing and bonding experience of shared work is almost completely absent. Often, the honing of maturity and skill takes place in things that can have value, like the lessons of sports, but in a more artificial and temporary form, not the mature form of craft, work, and responsibility, which is a way of life that one joins and stays in through maturity.

Often, parents find themselves searching out ways to create the feeling of responsibility through willpower and organization, but the reality of it often escapes them. And of course, there is the problem of abject and even sinful immaturity that is made possible by the lack of work and responsibility, wherein the innocence of childlike play is continued into adolescence and becomes the disorder of childish indulgence.

COMPETENCY

Alongside the patent immaturity of many adolescents today, there is a great emphasis on the need to communicate and create self-esteem. This desire is noble in that we want our children to sense their worth and place within society, and to be raised in confidence. But self-esteem is often reduced to information that is communicated and repeated so that a child feels valuable and worthy. It is awarded with tokens and words but without incarnational reality in visible and worthy accomplishments related to man's nature and family. Traditionally, in homesteading cultures, an individual came to sense and know their worth through *competency*. The self-esteem of know-how is not information but *experience*. Competency—learning how to do things well—not only builds character but provides tangible proof of ability to both society and the individual. We often flippantly say that one ought not to be forced to "prove" himself to others because people should just be accepted as they are. This has some truth to it, but the fuller truth is that we become who and what we are in real life, which includes the achievements and necessity of good work done for the sake of something good. It is in this gift of work that one "proves" not only that he *can* do something but that he *will* do it for the right reasons.

When one learns how to inhabit their own place and homes in an active way— building, fixing, tending—he experiences the dominion of man explicitly. This is unlike the passivity inherent in a home being merely a place of consumption, where all

products are purchased and all problems are fixed by hired help. This embedded passivity, in some ways, is childish since it is children who naturally and innocently enter the world without know-how but then gain competency and character as they gain necessary and worthwhile skills whose end and purpose are right before them.

Competency also directs and inspires children toward productive work that incorporates the broader economy and community. This know-how often contributes to healthy entrepreneurship in the young as well, as they find enterprises that, in their abundance, can be cultivated for the family first but then offered as a true and valuable product for their community.

We should not fear that the skills of a homestead will not be valued the way extracurricular activities are. As non-technical college degrees are losing value today, both among students and employers—and the need for practical skills like critical thinking, problem-solving, logic, and common sense are increasingly less common in the youth

of America—the homestead, with its realities, victories, and failures, is an ideal training ground for children, especially boys. Not a day passes where tangible obstacles are not presented: stubborn milk cows must be milked, weeds must be battled, and repairs made to tools and equipment. As our children near the transition from childhood to adulthood, we increasingly find our shops somewhat in disarray because of the children. However, the fruits of the mess are priceless (in hindsight) as they are taking the initiative to build new farm implements, housing for the rabbits, and bee boxes for swarms. Yes, we need to work on organization skills a bit, but the self-starting, matured, and entrepreneurial spirit being cultivated is an invaluable skill that is not as easily created in any other environment.

— 3 —

FROM TIME CLOCKS
TO SEASONS

"The endeavor [or work] sums up the most important tem-poral elements of the universal good—the satisfaction of physical needs so that man may, without hindrance, devote himself to the worship of God. In this highest of goods, which is eternal salvation, the needs of all men find their fulfillment."

—STEFAN CARDINAL WYSZYNKI[30]

Living a life on the homestead requires retuning our sense of work and integration. Although man is made to work, he is also made for more. The liturgy of the land tells us that man is formed in both his work and his ordered rest. To tune ourselves to the liturgy of the land, we will need to both recover a Catholic spirit of rest and redefine the very purpose of marking the time. This is harder than it seems since the logic of our work is largely out of tune by being out of sync with any sense of the seasons. Working with the land helps this recovery tremendously. But before tuning ourselves to our work, we have to recover the Catholic understanding of *rest*.

FROM SUNDAY

One of the most interesting things about learning to farm the land is that we tend to begin thinking about the work of the land and not its rest. But to be a good farmer

---

30 Stefan Cardinal Wyszynki, *All You who Labor: Work and the Sanctification of Daily Life* (Manchester, NH: Sophia Institute Press), 36.

usually means to reverse this. Your emphasis tends to be on the rest the land needs before it can produce. Good homesteaders think of cover crops and compost *before* planting and harvesting. Those skilled husbandmen that build fertility and maintain healthy herds of grazing animals, for example, speak of how long grass needs to rest from grazing, not how much grazing you can get out of it. God even commanded that the Israelites let their land rest from crops (see Ex 23:11).

While God calls us to work, we also know that our humanity requires rest. Something essential happens in rest. We're even oriented toward salvation, which is often likened to entering God's rest, which we do each Sunday and solemnity. Rest is more than relaxation or a respite from work. It is what re-creates us (the meaning of the word "recreation"). And while the homestead is clearly a place of intense work, a spirit of worldly overworking without rest is a grave danger to our souls that we might easily impose on the land too—maybe even our family.

Perhaps ironically to some, it is a world of increased efficiency in mass production that often turns the world into a place of total work, as the Thomistic philosopher Josef Pieper puts it. He unites our modern inability to stop working with our inability to have true Christian festivity. In his book *In Tune with the World,* he notes that tuning our hearts in this way presupposes an appreciation of not only nature but also work related to real rhythms and true needs: "Not all activity, not every kind of expenditure of effort and earning of money, deserves the name work. That should be applied only to the active—and usually also laborious—procurement of the things that are truly useful for living [i.e., not for profit alone]. And it is a good guess that only meaningful work can provide the soil in which festivity flourishes. Perhaps both work and celebration spring from the same root, so that when one dries up, the other withers."[31]

On a Catholic homestead, one seeks to unite work and celebration, which Pieper says comes from our appreciative and approving love for reality itself. This approval is the act of man, inwardly and outwardly through his festivity, responding to God's proclamation that creation is good, as He calls it in Genesis. Our proper response— our affirming response—is in agreement. "Yes, it is," we say by resting in and enjoying it. This we do each time we eat a meal. On the homestead, that meal likely took a lot of work by man, but when we sit down to enjoy it—to let the work come to "rest" in us

---

31 Josef Pieper, *In Tune with the World: A Theory of Festivity* (South Bend, IN: St. Augustine's Press, 1999), 4.

and become us—we say to God, "Bless us . . . and these *Thy gifts*." Good work creates a receptive spirit or rest in God. Even though we are expending effort, we are still receptive as God's children. This rest we do by our festivities, and Pieper claims that it is the Church alone that truly knows what festivity is because we receive the goods of the earth and offer them up to God, completing the true purpose of creation itself.

The worship of God cannot be imagined without a connection to the earth from which it gathers the necessary elements for the sacraments. "All worship is affirmation," says Pieper, "not only of God but also of the world."[32] Our work in creation is ordered to and nourished by our festive and joyful hearts. The true joy of man will always be in life from God, in the gift of His creation and salvation. Once again, the artificiality of today's attempted happiness through material goods and the constructs of man shows us how disappointing or sinful the artificial world of man can be. "Artificial holidays,"

---

32 Pieper, 37.

says Pieper, "claim that man, especially in the exercise of political power, is able to bring about his own salvation as that of the world."[33] For example, some want to intentionally make Earth Day a religious holiday,[34] which of course also goes in tandem with politically induced salvation for both man and planet—without God.

This is challenging because the world teaches us to see work as more or less a form of drudgery, a necessary evil that we slog through so we can enjoy the pleasures available only by purchase and indulgence once work has ceased. This is why the secular world lives *for Friday*, the time when work stops and partying begins. It lives in a cycle of expenditure through labor and indulgence through pleasure. Work is a transaction where we pay to play and play as our pay. But the Catholic lives not for Friday but *from Sunday*. Rest in God, true leisure, purifies and directs our work. Joseph Ratzinger helpfully reminds us that, in fact, the good of our work is fed by our rest, our sabbath. "To celebrate the sabbath means to celebrate the covenant. It means to return to the source and to sweep away all defilement that our work has brought with it. It also means going forth into a new world in which there will no longer be slaves and masters but only free children of God—into a world in which humans and animals and the earth itself will share together as kin in God's peace and freedom."[35]

Ratzinger described the exile of God's people into Babylon, recorded in the Old Testament, as a sort of "forced sabbath" that they had to endure precisely because they neglected the worship and rest of God and, therefore, were not freed by work but enslaved to it. This abusive relationship with work, he notes, is related to abuse of the land in that the land needed a rest from man's careless activity so that peace could be reestablished: "[The] people had rejected God's rest, its leisure, its worship, its peace, and its freedom, and so they fell into the slavery of activity. They brought the earth into slavery of their activity and thereby enslaved themselves. Therefore God had to give them the sabbath that they denied themselves. In their 'no' to the God-given rhythm of freedom and leisure they departed from their likeness to God and so did damage to the earth."[36]

---

33 Pieper, 62.

34 Paul Greenberg and Carl Safina, "The Case For Making Earth Day a Religious Holiday," *Time*, April 21, 2023, https://time.com/6273684/earth-day-religious-holiday/.

35 Joseph Ratzinger, *'In the Beginning...' A Catholic Understanding of the Story of Creation and the Fall,* (Grand Rapids, MI: William B. Errdmans Publishing Company), 31.

36 Ratzinger, 32.

ARRANGED TIMES

The entirety of the Catholic life is oriented toward eternity, but this happens in the reality of a temporal and finite world, and how we work with and alongside creation is a part of it. This is why when Saint Benedict sought to apply Saint Paul's simple command to "pray without ceasing," he laid out a rule of life that is, at its simplest, *an arrangement of time to meet the needs of both body and soul.* Benedict's rule is similar to the zeal and precision of a manager's organization of labor in a factory, but an abbot orders the time of his sons for the worship of God whereas the completely secular manager only orders time for worldly goods. Benedict brought prayer into the entire day by bringing order and rhythm to how a monk's time was spent. Brilliantly and prudently, Benedict of Nursia took into account our supernatural ends alongside our natural needs, so he left directions from everything to when work and prayer should be done to when food and naps should be taken. Unlike our modern world, which speaks of "spending" time like money, Benedict was intent on figuring out how time is *offered* as prayer and sacrifice to God.

The Benedictine spirit has gained momentum as a response to modern ills. Joseph Ratzinger took the name Benedict as pope for a reason. "The Benedict Option" was a pseudo-movement created by writer Rod Dreher in a book by that name, which emphasized intentional communities of Christians. Many thought it was about farming communes, but it was not. However, there is a truth there that the civilizational accomplishment of the Benedictines *was* in fact essentially agrarian. How could it not be? And the liturgy of the land, the life of farming and prayer, is in many ways an image and synthesis of our Western tradition. John Senior reminds us that Benedictine life isn't just one thing among others. By its longevity and life, it has proved the connection between the work of the hand on a farm and the work of the soul in worship: "St. Benedict's [Rule] is best understood as the spirituality of ordinary life, based upon the fact acknowledged by all the masters of the philosophia perennial [the perennial philosophy]—Plato, Aristotle, St. Thomas Aquinas—and the constant teaching of the Popes . . . [is that] the common experience of mankind is that the vast majority of men are farmers."[37]

The ordering of time in the liturgy of the land, therefore, is not truly the clock alone but the broader seasons of nature and of the Church pioneered and lived from the farm. In other words, we must recover our clocks and tune them to God.

---

37 John Senior, *The Restoration of Christian Culture* (Norfolk, VA: HIS Press, 2008), 98.

TUNING THE CLOCKS

Blessedly, clocks are a Catholic invention and tool. One of the ways to be liberated from the drudgery of the time clock is to turn it back to its original use. People use the denigration "you can't turn back time" to dismiss homesteading as backward-looking. It is true that homesteaders are adjusting the clock. "The question is not whether you can set back the clock," said John Senior. "Of course you can. Clocks are instruments to tell time; they don't create it."[38] We are simply recovering the *use* of time, therefore. Long before alarms alerted us that it was time to get ready to go to work, it was the monks that first pioneered the technology of the clock for the purpose of *prayer*. As Neil Postman points out in his book *Technopoly*, the clock moved from the hands of monks to the other, more controlling hands: "The clock had its origin in the Benedictine monasteries of the twelfth and thirteenth centuries. The impetus behind the invention was to provide a more or less precise regularity to the routines of the monasteries, which required, among other things, seven periods of devotion during the course of the day [the Divine Office]. . . . But what the monks did not foresee was that the clock is a means not merely of keeping track of the hours but also of synchronizing and controlling the actions of men."[39]

As Postman notes, our tools can be used by us or we can be used by them. Tools can be very disruptive. Without careful attention, "[tools] bid to *become* the culture."[40] This is the paradox of a clock, a thing to mark the time, being pulled from the place and purpose of prayer and used as perhaps the greatest means of control for the sake of mammon: "The paradox, the surprise, and the wonder are that the clock was invented by men who wanted to devote themselves more rigorously to God; it ended as the technology of greatest use to men who wished to devote themselves to the accumulation of money."[41]

For the Catholic homestead, the first reordering of time back to God and prayer is to reclaim time itself for God. This is done by having daily set times of prayer. As Hillarie Belloc famously said, speaking of a return to a land-based people, "When noon is Angelus time, the clock is right."[42] Our first order of business is time, and we have to

---

38 *Restoration*, 42.

39 Neil Postman, *Technopoly: The Surrender of Culture to Technology* (New York: Vintage Books, 1993), 15.

40 Postman, 28, emphasis in the original.

41 Postman, 15.

42 From K. L. Kenrick, *Flee to the Fields: The Faith and Works of the Catholic Land Movement*, (Norfolk, VA: HIS Press, 2003), 6.

make sure time does not just mean business but instead means an opportunity to pray. The "laymen's office" of the Angelus and the daily Rosary have been central to the life of farms and homesteads for centuries, and they immediately create a rhythm of the day around the incarnation and life of Our Lord. These Marian prayers, said in the midst of creation, remind us that God became incarnate and dwelled among the work and thorns of life like and with us.

Tied as they are to the history of the monasteries, the devotions of the Rosary and the Angelus mark and order the days much as the Divine Office does for religious orders. Praying the Psalms daily is a beautiful and ancient tradition, even for the laity, who, in places like England (when it was Catholic), prayed the *Little Office of the Blessed Virgin Mary* so often that memorizing it was common. If one is inclined, the fuller Divine Office itself also marks well the work of each day. Along with the Psalms generally, the traditional prayers and hymns of the Divine Office, which can be prayed throughout the day, also connect our natural work under the sun with our supernatural work under our Father's care. One hears pleas for God to "direct the work of our hands" in the early hours. Hymns during the day ask God to "put out the flames of strife" that are symbolized in the heat of the noonday sun. Later, as the sun sets, the hymns turn to the "setting of life" in death.

Expanding out, the next order of prayer comes from the intertwining of the seasons of the Church and the land, which are more intertwined than some realize. Both of us have found that the traditional calendar (of the Latin Mass) is more suited and connected to the natural cycles of nature. In that older calendar, there is a greater emphasis on asking God in specific seasons for help with planting, harvesting, and so on, especially through Ember Days, which were celebrated four times a year in accord with both natural and ecclesiastical seasons (Winter/Advent and Christmas, Winter and Early Spring/Lent, Late Spring/Easter, and Summer/Pentecost). They were instated as means of both thanking God for the previous season and petitioning Him for the coming one. They were, therefore, fittingly penitential and grateful at the same time. Farming tends to make one feel penitential and grateful at the same time.

The natural and supernatural seasons often came with a beautiful harmony. Early spring, for example, coincides with Lent for the northern hemisphere as a season that sees the "bottom of the barrel," a time when meager meals were a natural necessity for the common family to get through until the first spring greening. In Appalachia and other places, the time when the leaves are coming out just before Easter is called the "hunger months," even if it is a beautiful time of year, based on the fact that seasonal abundance is *almost here but not yet.* This reinforces Lenten senses. The joys of Easter can be more fittingly celebrated because, with the new growth in the pasture and new animals being born, one could have more abundant dairy dishes and lamb for the feast. The joys and harvest of Pentecost stretch toward the fall as the planted seeds are harvested, just as the Church, in that season, enjoyed the fruitful harvest made possible by the Holy Ghost. And as the season inches toward the death of winter, the feasts of All Souls and All Saints remind us of that end before we await the hope that winter is pregnant with during Advent and Christmastide. This reality of feasting, fasting, and seasonal variety intimately and naturally tied societies to the land, the seasons, the local culture, and their liturgy.

DAYS OF PLANTING AND HARVEST

As the daily devotional life of a Catholic is marked by a daily rhythm (like the Angelus and Rosary) and a seasonal rhythm (like the liturgical year), so too a homestead has daily chores and seasonal chores. Learning to recognize and integrate those works, and letting them shape your home's culture, is something that will need to be learned early on.

Most of us are formed with a more industrial mindset, which is one of constant, uninterrupted production. Natural cycles are reduced, removed, and overcome by technology whenever possible. This is not so with the liturgy of the land.

Daily chores include the more demanding and regular work, usually of livestock. Feeding animals, letting hens out and putting them back up, milking cows, and moving animals to new paddocks—all of these things are fairly regular. Even on a small scale, however, these simple tasks can have a huge impact on keeping you connected to your homestead, helping you root into it as a way of life. As we'll discuss later, decisions on which enterprises you engage in will be shaped by how deeply you want your life to be impacted by the homesteading life. Though daily and demanding, these regular chores can be integrated into a more modern lifestyle if needed. In rural areas, many old-timers talk about milking the cow before hopping on a school bus to town.

Seasonal work, as the name suggests, is not as regular and, therefore, requires a different sort of planning and attention. It is often related to plants—hay, harvesting crops, and gathering fruit. Historically, food was primarily a local and seasonal affair before refrigeration and artificial preservation, which reinforced the connection to the natural

seasons. Larders, fermentation, drying, smoking, or salting did offer some shelf exten-sion for staples. However, the rest of the farmer's diet was largely sourced from fresh ingredients. Berries, birds, fruits, and greens in the summer. Grains, gourds, game, and nuts in the fall. Roots and the slaughtering of the fattened hog or calf in the early winter. These activities shape the culture of a homestead because these big moments of sowing, reaping, and preserving are the literal life of the home and also the life of the culture. We have often found that because we approach them alongside our family, we should be attentive to marking these times and not miss the opportunity of enjoying them and letting them shape our lives.

The difference in seasonal demands of various enterprises will shape what and how you homestead. People that have summers off, like teachers, might enjoy gardening or beekeeping more than a milk cow. Someone who works from home in a very steady and unchanging work might be able to make a significant investment of time in a milk cow. But the seasons and work shape you either way.

Bee Seasons

– Tommy Van Horn

Having spent most of my life in the Deep South, the concept of seasons was often vague. Our hot and humid summers would transition to a slightly less hot but still humid fall, followed by two days of winter and back to a less hot but still humid spring. It wasn't until I began keeping bees for a hobby and then as a livelihood that the distinctions of the seasons, even in the Deep South, became more apparent. Rather than measuring a season by degrees of misery, I began to see, what was once invisible to my jaded eye, a hidden beauty in the landscape and plant life: the first Maple bloom in January, the greening of a Tupelo tree in March, or the "goldening" of Golden Rod in September. Noticing these subtle distinctions in the context of my craft of beekeeping brought not only a new awareness of the natural world where I lived and worked but also a love of place as described by Wendell Berry.

One of the biggest shifts in daily life when moving toward a land-based lifestyle was the constraint seasons placed on our work and life. Yet we have learned to welcome the limitations they impose on us when coming from essentially a limitless world of global trade, manufacturing, and information technology. We dove into beekeeping on a commercial scale, and working bees has a tremendous variation of

work requirements. The summers can be grueling in hot, humid air, especially inside a bee suit! And winters can bring everything to a near-total halt. We have been inclined to even say, "I want more winter!"

Being finite beings ourselves, it seems there is something deep within us in need of limitations, and when we accept those realities on the homestead rather than force our will, the work is not only more fruitful but also comes with greater ease. We learned from the bees to see the limits and times of the seasons as something beautiful and instructive. Making up new bee colonies too late in the summer or fall will certainly mean they perish over the winter; there is just no way around forcing them to grow in time. Spring greens grow best in mild weather, and tomatoes do best in the summer warmth. Even the wild deer instinctively know when it's best to breed and birth their young based on the abundance of seasonal resources. Working within these confines providentially brings freedom and peace of mind, knowing everything doesn't have to be done right now but rather lets the seasons and the rhythm of natural cycles dictate work and leisure.

After winter, the bees begin bringing in pollen and nectar from Elm and Maple trees in our area well before spring is visible to most. The hive begins to expand with the incoming resources, and within a matter of weeks, the colony wants to reproduce itself in phenomena called Swarming. This typically only occurs in the spring or early summer when the bees instinctively know there is abundance and they are months away from the following winter, so there is time to reproduce and still collect enough resources for the colony to survive the winter dearth later in the year. As a beekeeper collaborating with nature, we use this swarm instinct to our advantage. Every spring, we go through each colony and take half the bees and honey, creating an artificial swarm, then place this new split in a different beehive with a new queen. We replace any colonies that perished from the previous year this way or sell any surplus splits for additional income. That's all we are focused on for about four to six weeks; we are not worried about making honey or treating for disease or building new equipment. By the end of that four-to-six-week period, my neck is sore from looking down, my shoulders ache, and I feel cross-eyed from staring at thousands of frames of bees, but I know that task is complete for the year and soon there is a lull in the work before the task of making honey starts in the summer. It was hard to adjust to at first, but focusing intensely on seasonal tasks yields better results for the land, the bees, and even my family.

— 4 —

FROM ARTIFICIAL
TO NATURAL

"The first ground of hope is the undeniable instinct to have a family. The mere erotic relation of male and female is not the be-all and end-all of social life; in spite of the scented literature which so often offers deodorants as disinfectants. So native to the heart of man and woman is it to have a home, and therefore a quiver-full of children that much money and all kinds of literary best-sellers have been moderately successful against it. Naturam expelles furca, tamen usque recurret (You can drive nature out with a pitchfork, but back she comes)."

—FR. VINCENT MCNABB, OP[43]

As we speak of moving to a homestead as a form of *conversion*, of learning the liturgy of the land, it is worth starting with examining what exactly we are moving away from and what we are moving toward. We propose that what drives people away from modern life and toward the tradition of homesteading is a gnawing dislike of the *artificial* and a greater desire for the *natural*. This could be understood as a spectrum—not necessarily opposing forces, though they can be. As Father McNabb pointed out in the opening quote, the impulse toward family and, therefore, children (and he would also argue toward homesteading) is not a matter of mechanical ideas of utopian order but an impulse of human nature itself.

---

43   Vincent McNabb, *Old Principles and the New Order* (Providence, RI: Cluny), 95.

MADE BY MAN

When we hear the word "artificial," we might consider it in a negative sense. It is true that in modern use, it can mean something like duplicitous or fake. And we acknowledge and propose that our artificiality has slipped into a way of life that is dangerous. However, when theologians like Saint Thomas Aquinas use the word, they are simply designating something made by man. Things made by man are not in essence evil, because man was created good. To understand artificial in a good sense, we can remember that it has the root *art*, as in created by human hands. Today, we designate something made by a skilled person as something *artisan*. Similarly, we can call something an artifact to designate it as something made by man in antiquity.

The art of man, therefore, is the work of man. Birds and beasts do not make art in a strict sense. In its most basic sense, the use of art is how we, as man, use what is provided naturally through creation to answer for both our body's need for food and shelter and our soul's need for truth, beauty, and goodness. A home, for example, "is caused to be in matter by *art* alone," says Aquinas.[44] But having a soul that needs warmth as well, our homes are said to be warm by their very environment, the people, artwork, and way of life. Our higher arts, such as music and paintings, are not disconnected from the lower arts, such as farming and craft, but are built up from them.

There are plentiful and worthwhile calls for Catholics to renew a culture in decline. We, of course, do that in legitimately cultural ways: through our art, music, and so on. Our art should and does reach upward toward the heavens, lifting up eyes and hearts. But we Catholics have also treasured what can be called the basic arts, which are also beautiful and humanizing if we have eyes to see and can enjoy them for what they are. These arts, those that connect more directly to the simple life of a family and a home, make up the work and culture of a homestead. There's something very reasonable in returning to the soil to build upward toward a true culture. The high cultures the Catholics have enjoyed, it can be argued, cannot be resuscitated without some connection to these elemental arts—from the ground up if you will.

---

44 *Summa Theologica*, I, q. 117, art. 1.

HIGH AND LOW ART

Many have argued well that our society actually cannot be culturally renewed toward truth, beauty, and goodness without a genuine return to foundations in nature. John Francis Nieto has written about older forms of life that were, in fact, built from nature and therefore had the potential to be a true and humane culture, whereas our modern life is not only distant from nature but built up *without* it:

> For many reasons, we cannot hunt, sew, sing, farm, cook, dance, or wash clothes as could those who have lived in villages until very recently. We have exchanged such abilities for many advantages, especially long lives and material possessions. I propose here that the loss is much greater than the gain—in some sense it is infinite. I propose that we have lost the inter-action with nature that allows us to cultivate our own, human, nature in a manner conducive to happiness—by which I mean true, human thriving and fulfillment—not merely living, but living well, the good life.[45]

45 John Francis Nieto, "Nature and Art in the Village," *The Josias*, February 1, 2017, https://thejosias.com/2017/02/01/nature-and-art-in-the-village/.

Clearly, living more naturally for the Catholic homesteader is not just a matter of enjoying the fresh air but of being able to live a fully human life and build up a true and beautiful culture. Therefore, we might only be able to build upward to high culture by learning again the lessons of low culture, like building and growing things—work integrated with nature and its lessons and limits.

In Wendell Berry's short story *The Art of Loading Brush*, an old man named Andy Catlett is very intentionally—even forcefully—trying to communicate this connection between the high and low arts of man. In the story, Andy has recently hired (and fired) a fence crew to fix an old fence on his family farm. Their work was done, but it was done shoddily and messily—without care and love, for profit alone. To clean up after them, the old man hires a college student named Austin who is home on summer break. The boy, who is in intense training in the arts of music, is now being trained in the art of farming.

They set to the first thing, which is loading brush. It doesn't take long before Austin gets the main thrust of that morning's lesson. After tossing in "with a young athlete's depreciating nonchalance," Andy calls out for him to stop. "We ain't going to make a mess to clean up a mess," Andy says. "Do you want to put one load into three loads or into one load?" He goes on to challenge a whole society, though he is talking only to Austin, to rethink its inability and unwillingness to appreciate the lower arts:

> Now, he said, "We're practicing the art of loading brush. It is a fundamental art. An indispensable art. Now I know about your 'fine arts,' your music and literature and all that—I've been to school too—and I'm telling you they're optional. The art of loading brush is not optional."
>
> "You talking about symphonies?" Austin had stopped and was standing still to signify the importance of symphonies.

Andy goes on to use some rather colorful language to communicate that, yes, he's talking about symphonies too. After making that clear, Andy communicates the main lesson of the day, which is founded in brush but reaches up much higher. Today, there is something fundamental we need to recover. "And in my opinion," Andy says, "if the art of loading brush dies out, the art of making music finally will die out too. You tell

your professors, when you go back, that you met an old provincial man, a leftover, who told you: No high culture without low culture, and when low culture is the scarcest it is the highest."[46]

Our quest for the natural—for the real—through homesteading can be seen as a response, a realization, that the arts related more directly to nature have become the highest need. This is because the arts of man seem to have slipped away into something dangerous for our homes and souls; the arts in the good sense have been lost to the artificial in the bad sense and bad taste. Traditionally, for example, works of art were meant to communicate the beauty and truth of the world, but as art has moved more and more into the realm of the abstract and is used primarily to express the individuality of the artist himself, that art can become grotesque and even evil simply because it has forgotten

---

46 Wendell Berry, *The Art of Loading Brush* (Berkeley, CA: Counterpoint, 2017), 254–56.

God. It is no longer a reflection and communication of the good, true, and beautiful—transcendent in the connection to what God has given and man has cultivated in that gift—but reflects man alone. As we depart from what God has made and possess only what man has made, then we are more and more left with the only thing that man has really "created" solely from his own being, which is sin.

Something too artificial can replace or displace our contact with what is real. All art is attractive insofar as it relates to us something essentially human, something good and real. But it can grow too distant, retaining something attractive to us yet also being an abuse or disorder of the truly good. Social media, for example, is an artifact of man that is only popular and consumed because it comes from man's need for social living. But when it becomes completely dislodged from reality in practice, or if it *replaces* the authentic and natural need for sociability, which is contact with people as a whole (in person), it can become disordered or evil. It can destroy the man as it purports to fulfill a need of the man. Many of us have seen and sensed this, even without philosophical analysis.

The great danger of moving away from what is *real* is that the limits, lessons, and purpose of real things get obscured or divided. God communicates Himself through real things, through nature, and we have a harder time hearing and sensing God's communication if we're too distanced from them. As Joseph Ratzinger put it:

> In the technological world, which is a self-made world of man, one does not immediately encounter the Creator; rather, initially, it is only himself that always encounters. The fundamental structure of this world is feasibility, and the manner of its certainty is the certainty of what can be calculated. Therefore even the question of salvation is not geared to God, who appears nowhere; rather, once again it is geared toward the ability of man, who wants to become the engineer of himself and history. . . . For him, creation is silent with regard to morality; it speaks only the language of mathematics, of technological utility, or else it protests against violation by man.[47]

---

47 Joseph Ratzinger, *Handing on the Faith in an Age of Disbelief* (San Francisco: Ignatius, 2006), 14.

OF WARMTH AND WOOD

Man lives from the earth, as he was created from it. And as co-creator working with creation, man is, in a sense, an extension of God; we rely on the strength of mind and body that comes from Him. Tools are but an extension of man's strength and intellect applied to gathering and using the earth's goods. But there is clearly a danger if the tools completely sever us from the world, just as we can be severed from God. Now, lest we be accused of being unthinking Luddites, we should acknowledge that the genius of man can be seen in his machines. We might even call it an art. But our arts cannot be severed wholly from the nature from which they spring up or we may simply lose sight of what is real, what comes from God. In some ways, the excess of industrialism and technology is just that: the use of genius in such a way that severs it from reality itself.

Romano Guardini reflected on this danger. He seemed to think, like others, that to slip away from our closer need and use of nature is to actually slip from good, true, and beautiful human culture into something dangerously artificial. He examines how technology can displace our work with nature because he sees man as truly himself only when working close to creation. "Only in this way can any work of culture, of mind and spirit, be done."[48] Thinking of the use of wood for heat, he points us to how the use of wood in the home is both function and culture; it is body and soul:

> In older Italian houses, especially in rural areas, you will always find the open hearth. We have here something that is bound up with the deepest roots of human existence: seizing open fire and putting the flame to use to warm us. Mind and spirit are at work here; nature is put to human use, and an element of human existence is achieved. There is a payment in some remoteness from nature, to be sure. I am aware of the roar of a fire and the primitive power of uncontrolled flamed. Here we have a softening and thinning out and distancing. That is the cost of culture. But nature is still close at hand. . . . This is human living. With some exaggeration we might say that being human means lighting a fire at a protected spot so that it may give light and heat.[49]

48 Romano Guardini, *Letters from Lake Cuomo: Explorations in Technology and the Human Race* (Grand Rapids, MI: William B. Eerdmans, 1994).
49 Guardini, 14.

The "cost of culture" is what we use from nature, making it for our humanity, but still connected to what is real. This is, to Guardini, what true human culture is. He contrasts this with the thermostat: "[Think] of heating by electricity, in which nothing burns at all, but a current comes into the house and gives warmth in some way. The manifestation of culture has gone, the link with nature has been cut, a totally artificial situation has been created. Everything that was achieved by human existence before an open fire is a thing of the past."[50]

He laments the situation because the snapped link between nature, work, and culture seems to be both unstoppable in its production of things and destructive in its cost to human culture. "The sphere in which we live is becoming more and more artificial, less and less human, more and more—I cannot help saying it—barbarian."[51]

The danger seems to be that technology today has created its own logic, a principle we live from instead of living from creation itself. The word "technology," which is so dominate in today's discourses, actually comes from uniting the Greek word *techne*, which means something akin to technique, with the word *logos,* where we get the word "logic" from. And, interestingly, the word *logos* is the same word Saint John used to describe Jesus Christ, the Word (or *logos*) of God that became flesh and dwelled among us (see Jn 1). Technology today is so all-encompassing as to seem to have its own *logos,* its own word that has come from man and replaced the Word that has come from God. Marx said we are determined by our instruments, and we should be wary that he might be right. Our concern here is not with technology per se but with it insofar as it distances us from a reality that we need to experience to grow in wisdom and virtue.

The classical educator John Senior, famous for inspiring a whole generation of Catholic projects and cultural endeavors, was wary and fearful of what our distance from reality did to us. Without regular contact with reality, he argued, we were simply unformed or even deformed because God Himself has ordered creation to communicate truth through contact with nature. Without contact with real things, love for real things never formed and the things of God became an annoyance in this false garden of Eden. Like Guardini, he too lamented the loss of the hearth, of the family gathered around a fire. In his essay *The Air Conditioned Holocaust*, he deftly dismantles the harm

---

50 Guardini, 23.
51 Guardini, 25.

done by all of the techniques and errors of modern man, but instead of engaging the lunatics, he recommended a retreat back to reality around the fire: "Families don't draw their chairs up closer to the central heating duct. . . . Build a fireplace. . . . Smash the television set, turn out the lights, build a fire in the fireplace, move the family into the living room, put a pot on to boil some tea and toddy and have an experiment in merriment, a sudden unexpected hearth, the heart and first step in the restoration of the home."[52]

Senior's former student and biographer, Fr. Francis Bethel, OSB, noted that Senior consistently pointed to the rural and homesteading life as a way of grounding oneself in reality amid so much artificiality. This is what gives it such importance today. "We know that Senior always lived in the country while teaching," Father Bethel remembers. "He had noticed the profit that came to Mark Van Doren [his mentor] from growing up on a farm and, as a teacher, living and working part of the year in a rustic context." Senior kept a milk cow, for example, and was never shy about his disdain for industrialism, simply because he valued the goods of the soul more than the body. The hard fact about industrialization is that it has so thoroughly taken man from the context and lessons of the homestead: "[The] chilling truth is that industrialism brings a paralyzing gluttony and greed in which the quality of life is quantified. Paradoxically, you cannot afford to have children in an affluent society. The world has never been so rich and wretched as in these air-conditioned Edens where another child would sap the payments on the second car."[53]

Life on a homestead—where the home lives in the context of working alongside nature—provides a beautiful means of coming to such truth because God made creation in a way that reveals the Creator. Put differently, there are things we cannot know outside of contact with nature. Therefore, being surrounded and ordered by an artificial, technological, man-made world—especially as that mode of life is made even more artificial by living online and through media—leaves a void in our own ability to come to know the truth. As Saint Bonaventure said, "If there is anyone who is not enlightened by this sublime magnificence of created things, he is blind. . . . If there is anyone who, seeing all these works of God, does not praise him, he is dumb; if there is anyone who, from so many signs, cannot perceive God, that man is foolish."

---

52 John Senior, *The Restoration of Christian Culture* (Norfolk, VA: IHS Press), 48.
53 John Senior, *The Death of Christian Culture* (Norfolk, VA: IHS Press, 2008), 24.

Surely, we live in a time of foolishness, a time that doesn't see God in nature because it doesn't see nature. We are even told that the great discoveries made through the scientific study of nature have made God *less* perceivable, but anyone who is in actual contact with nature, seeing, living, and working alongside it, knows that the opposite is true. Quite regularly, our children are literally stopped in their tracks during our early morning chores by the splendor of a sunrise or struck upon returning from milking on a winter night when the beauty of the stars cannot be ignored. At such times, one can easily relate to the perception of God in those moments, as when David cried out in the Psalms, "When I look at your heavens, . . . the stars which you have established; what is man that you are mindful of him?" (Ps 8:3–4).

CHAPTER

— 5 —

FROM ARTIFICIAL ECONOMY TO NATURAL ECONOMY

"If more of us valued food and cheer and song above hoarded gold, it would be a merrier world."

–J. R. R. TOLKIEN

"Even if a man sees, as I see, that the Bible, and especially the Gospels, are the world's best handbook of Economics, he will have surprises almost every time he opens the book."

–FR. VINCENT MCNABB, OP[54]

Surely, as we speak of moving toward the homestead, we must consider the economic realities of it. But this too often moves immediately to paying for things, not making and growing things, which, along with the spiritual health of the family, are the principal ends of Catholic homesteading. There is a general discomfort in the modern mind of thinking of God providing for us in the ways He made clear He would—food and shelter—so we move immediately to care only in the form of money, the dominant valuation of wealth.

We will treat some of the economic realities as related to wages and money, but to do that—to have the conversion to the homestead—we must recover an understanding of what Saint Thomas Aquinas calls natural economy, which is the basic economy of the homestead. This is a requirement for living the liturgy of the land.

---

54 Vincent McNabb, *Nazareth or Social Chaos* (Norfolk, VA: HIS Press, 2009), 13.

The secular world, which has so thoroughly dismissed the centrality of God and family, simply cannot speak intelligently about the economy because they don't know how to speak of the family, the reality of things, and what they even mean by "value." As Joseph Pearce puts it: "The most fundamental flaw in the way that economic growth is measured is linked inextricably to the worship of price mechanism. The slavery of economists to the omnipotent Market has resulted in their linking the rate of growth to 'gross national product' (GNP). . . . And, since growth is always considered good, the more that GNP increases the more economists will speak of a 'healthy economy' and the more politicians will preen themselves on their success in bringing it about."[55]

And he notes that home-based, productive, and multigenerational work is not even measured by economists, meaning they see it as worthless: "Preparing meals at home is less 'economic' than eating at a restaurant. . . . Similarly, all do-it-yourself economics around the home or on the car are in fact 'uneconomic.' . . . Caring for the elderly or disabled people at home within a loving family environment, where they are largely invisible economically, is less 'economic' than having their 'price' measured in a nursing home."[56]

This is simply because GNP is artificial and unnatural. Because it is increasingly distanced from nature, it points only to man, often only the individual man. Part of seceding from economic evils will be to reconnect the purpose of work and wealth with the direct care of the family in more ways than just funding it and in submitting to God's abundant directives on how wealth ought to be used.

Natural wealth, by contrast, is defined as being "related to household management," says Aquinas, "not as an end, but as something ordered to an end, which is *the management of the home*."[57] "Natural wealth is that which serves man as a remedy for his natural wants," says Fr. George H. Speltz in speaking of Aquinas's teaching, such as food, shelter, clothing, and so on. These are not just material things and, therefore, unimportant. Filling these natural needs is the duty and vocation of man. To fail in this regard is not just a material failure but a spiritual failure as well. As Saint Paul says, he who doesn't care for his family is "worse than an unbeliever" (1 Tm 5:8).

---

55 Joseph Pearce, *Small is Still Beautiful: Economics as if Families Mattered* (Wilmington, DE: ISI Books, 2006), 21.

56 Pearce, 21.

57 Quoted in George Speltz, *The Importance of the Rural Life According to the Philosophy of St. Thomas Aquinas* (Scotts Valley, CA: CreateSpace Publishing, 2011), 82.

Notice that natural wealth is always related to "natural wants." This would, therefore, not include things of *luxury*, though natural wealth can be had in abundance. Virtuous and natural abundance, however, is always designated as natural by its *purpose*, which is the care of a family and neighbors. This is why we can say accurately and not analogously that a rich man estranged from his family lacks true wealth—that is, natural wealth—even if he can buy whatever he wants with his money. He is truly poor.

ARTIFICIAL TOOLS

The natural economy does have exchange because it seems to be part of the designs of God that man, by needing to provide for natural needs but not being able to produce *everything* himself, is brought into practical society with his neighbor. Bartering, for example, exchanges natural wealth for natural wealth to provide for the needs of our created nature. This is still a natural economy and a form of natural wealth, and given its closeness to nature and neighbor, it carries many opportunities for virtue and dissuades us from wealth-related vices simply because we would have to face our sins in the face of a friend or neighbor.

But given the difficulty and complexity of always using bartered goods in these necessary exchanges, man has invented money as a tool to hold the place of the value of these goods. The use of money, which is an old tool of man, creates the opportunity to *value the money itself*, disconnected from the natural purposes of things themselves. Money thus creates a different sort of wealth—artificial wealth. Aquinas defines it this way: "Artificial wealth is that which is not a direct help to nature, as money, but is invented by the art of man, for the convenience of exchange, and as a measure of things saleable."[58] Clearly, homesteaders still engage in the artificial economy and will need to be responsible and wise with the usefulness of money as a tool, but we can understand much of their work and effort to be means of *displacing* the need for the artificial economy—money—by producing things directly. Most homesteaders will require some off-farm work, and this should not be seen as some sort of violation of the principles of homesteading, as if the choices are only all artificial or all-natural. The economic order of the world makes that very difficult. But being more closely connected to what is natural, economically speaking, keeps our work quite literally

---

58 *Summa Theologica*, I-II, q. 2, art. 1.

grounded in that which is most important to us, especially living virtuously for the glory of God and the good of our family.

DANGERS OF ARTIFICIAL WEALTH

Artificial wealth and the tool of money can be used by man in a virtuous way. Our Lord made use of money. But there are dangers present with it, as we shouldn't forget that it was Judas who kept the money that the apostles used when needed (see John 12:6).

According to Aquinas, artificial economies have significant moral dangers that are not as prevalent in natural ones. This is why he warns us against an economy built entirely on what he calls trade. Trade, according to Aquinas, denotes "wealth-getting" by *money from money*, the end of the work being money to build wealth, not things to satisfy needs. Unlike natural economic activity that sells what is produced for money to be used on other goods, trade simply buys low and sells high, as they say, and therefore creates a form of profiting that is more disconnected from ends and apt to make all things into money instead of making money with things.

Someone who increases value or wealth by *making or growing things* is more connected to true and good ends. For example, one who makes and sells chairs to his community is connected to the things (or ends) of the chair and the person that needs somewhere to sit. The profit he makes is a reward for answering a true need. Someone who *trades* in chairs might not care about the chair or the customer, because the reason

for purchasing the chair was to sell it. Jesus seemed more than displeased with those who were buying and selling and the money changers in the temple. Without these ends being a part of the economy and work of a person, the tendency toward excess or abstraction is keen because there is no end to the making of money. You don't know when you are "done" the way you do when you make a chair and then sell it.

By satisfying human needs directly and naturally—through work and exchange—one has a sense of satisfaction and completion. The end is clear and present. Perhaps with some irony, the gaining of money apart from the true necessities of life, instead of breeding contentment, can cultivate dissatisfaction, as Aquinas notes: "There are some who are never satisfied with what they have and always want more. This is a lack of moderation [temperance], since desire should always be measured according to one's needs: 'Give me neither beggary nor riches; give me the necessities of life' (Prov 30:8)."[59]

Pointing out the potential disorder of unnatural wealth does not dismiss that it could serve some good purpose. It is clearly true that many have an abundance of material wealth and are generous with it, but that generosity, according to Catholic teaching, is something bound on them by God and not merely their free choice.

Aquinas acknowledges that there is a limited need for trade, but he has a warning for societies that displace all natural economies with artificial economies, those that are animated by a constant purpose of wealth-getting. Surely, we can see these insights as prophetic:

> Again, if the citizens themselves devote their lives to matters of trade, the way will be opened up to many vices. For, since the object of tradesmen leads especially to making money, greed is awakened in the hearts of the citizens through the pursuit of trade. The result is that everything in the city will be offered for sale: confidence will be destroyed and the way opened to all kinds of trickery: each one will work only for his profit, despising the public good; the cultivation of virtue will fail, since honour, virtue's reward, will be bestowed upon anybody. Thus, in such a city civic life will necessarily be corrupted.[60]

---

59 Quoted in Speltz, *The Importance of the Rural Life*, 96.
60 Speltz, 96.

In other words, the potential of vice comes from valuing all things for the money itself and what it can do, not its proper end and use. And such valuation can easily slide into other excesses, disorders, and sins. This is essentially what happened to Judas. "'Why was this ointment not sold for three hundred denarii and given to the poor?' This he said, not that he cared for the poor but because he was a thief, and as he had the money box he used to take what was put into it" (Jn 12:5–6).

The antidote for this disorder is not merely in limiting the practice and presence of "tradesmen," though it certainly includes that, but in reconnecting the true and natural purpose of all economic activity, which is the good of families in relation to one another through society and local culture. Work and profit related to a home have a built-in limitation, or temperance, says Aquinas, unlike seeking wealth for its own sake: "Wealth-getting seeks wealth without limit, whereas household management *seeks it in a limited degree*."[61] These limits, like personal self-mastery, are a necessary part of directing the power and ability of man toward good ends.

The homesteader has contact not only with the natural world more broadly but also with the natural economy—the value of things for their proper end and use, which is not in status, monetary value, or any other worldly honor but solely in their relationship to the care of those we care about. In short, we have made money a god simply because we have made something finite into something infinite; we can never seem to have enough money. This is very different from the world of real things that proposes limits to us not arbitrarily but so that we might actually find contentment in this world and be able to see beyond the finite to what is actually infinite. As Fr. Vincent McNabb, OP, put it: "The very fulness of their reality limits man's desire. No man, unless at enmity with his reason, desires infinte things. If food is needed, no man desires an infinite meal; if clothing, no man desires an infinite garment; if shelter, no man desires an infinite house; if possessions, no man desires an infinite to till. Man's being and powers of doing have a bound which sets a limit to the things he needs."[62]

INTEGRATED ECONOMIES

The Catholic homestead is a place not of endless churn and striving but of contended and peaceful work integrated with nature and family. Not only is a natural economy

---

61 Quoted in Speltz, 82, emphasis added.
62 McNabb, *Nazareth or Social Chaos*, 15.

truly sustainable, but it is the happiness of man because it is man working and living in accord with the created nature of the world, and nature includes the economies of man, which means the households of man. Ultimately, therefore, a natural economy is one submitted to the spiritual and natural laws of God.

To focus on the homestead in this way is not to dismiss the fact that many of us will still engage with the economy of money and artificial wealth but to note that the beginning of any movement toward the land is not in switching to farming as an occupation—most people simply don't have the resources or experience for such a switch—but in submitting the world's artificial economy to God's natural economy instead of the other way around. Given the sheer dominance of the globalizing economy, this will happen only with effort and intention. Simply put, homesteading submits what is artificial to what is natural as a tool instead of submitting what is natural to what is artificial to get rich. Or, as one old saying goes, we want to eat what we can sell instead of sell what we can eat.

As the homestead is the natural habitat for family life, so too the natural economy is what grows organically from the homestead. The man of Psalm 128 describes such a life well:

> Blessed is every one who fears the Lord,
> who walks in his ways!
>
> You shall eat the fruit of the labor of your hands;
> you shall be happy, and it shall be well with you.
>
> Your wife will be like a fruitful vine
> within your house;
>
> your children will be like olive shoots
> around your table.
>
> Lo, thus shall the man be blessed
> who fears the Lord.
>
> The Lord bless you from Zion!
> May you see the prosperity of Jerusalem
> all the days of your life!
>
> May you see your children's children!
> Peace be upon Israel! (Ps 128)

He enjoys the food he grows with his family—to "eat the fruit of the labor." His family is fruitful. His children are no burden, not just mouths to feed, because they too will integrate into the work of the home, helping it to be more abundant by applying themselves to the act and culture of providing; they bring more, not less. Family meals are like a sacramental and sign of the goodness of this life, the delight of husband, wife, and kids. The integration and care for a specific place, in this case, Jerusalem, is a delight to see. And there is a presumption of longevity through multiple generations working together in the fruitful work of a home—"your children's children."

This life of work, abundance, food, shelter, family, generations, local community, and religion is a *wealthy* life. Whenever Sacred Scripture speaks of the wealth of a father and his household, this is the sense of wealth it means. When the kings of Israel actually obeyed God, the Hebrews were able to leave the battlefields and enslavements of other nations to enjoy contentment and rest in the provision of the land: "And Judah and Israel dwelt in safety, from Dan even to Beer-sheba, every man under his vine and under his fig tree" (1 Kgs 4:25).

Our First Milk Cows
–Jason Craig

When we first started homesteading, it was part dream and part demand. The dream was there because our family was growing, my studies in graduate school alerted me to the decline of the family, and we disliked living in an apartment in a city. These things made it very clear to us that we needed to be on the land. The demand was forced upon us because we didn't have money. Real estate problems from the 2008 economic crisis combined with a suspension of pay from my employer left us quite literally penniless. So we needed to get to the land because we just couldn't stomach the city anymore, but also because we needed a place to grow food just to save some money.

Providentially, we found a homestead situated on a larger piece of land owned by multiple generations that we could live on in exchange for labor. Though there were some downsides, we were able to really try out many different things, from poultry to forestry to cattle. Having many acres of pasture to make use of (if we kept it mowed), we decided on milk cows. We actually spent our last little bit of cash on two jersey cows. Now, over a decade later, we milk cows on a micro-commercial scale, meaning a licensed commercial operation but infinitesimally smaller than most dairy farms today. We are fully and totally a dairy family, and it shapes the culture of our homestead more than anything else.

But those two cows could have ended in disaster. They had never been milked, and we had never milked a cow. After they calved, there were two weeks of what felt like some of the hardest days we've ever had farming. First, one of them was terrible to train, and to this day, she is the first one to kick you. Going from never touching a cow to getting kicked by one was quit the transition. Second, the reality of this endless chore—milking twice a day, every day—was like an initiation into a wholly different way of life. Third, we were hand-milking in a barn about one hundred yards from where we were living, which meant walking clean buckets there every day and hauling milk back, cleaning in the house, and then doing it all over again. It was serious work of an order we had never known before. And this is without all of the other headaches that aren't as challenging now but were then: cows escaping a fence, training stubborn calves on a bottle, dealing with mastitis in the cows, and so on.

The two observations from this that really shaped how I viewed the natural economy described by Aquinas relate to need and value.

We stuck with it because we needed it. Multiple dairy farmers had given us discouraging advice that I would sum up as, "Don't do it, and when you can't do it, quit."

But the need to provide for our family demanded that we figure it out and endure. Had quitting been more of an option, it is hard to say how it would have ended. When you really need your homestead, your decisions are very different.

The next observation, or lesson, was that the land was making us feel like we were living like royalty. After making it through some of the early difficulties, we were swimming in the highest quality milk we had ever tasted. We had butter, yogurt, ghee, cheese, and even ice cream. We strained out the whey to use in fermentation. We used the manure in the garden. We sat in peace with the cows in the pasture. We slaughtered the calves for meat. The abundance, taste, and satisfaction of that first major homesteading endeavor changed how we understood value and wealth.

— 6 —

FROM WAGES TO PRODUCTIVE PROPERTY

"It is surely undeniable that, when a man engages in remu-
nerative labor, the impelling reason and motive of his work is
to obtain property, and thereafter to hold it as his very own.
If one man hires out to another his strength or skill, he does
so for the purpose of receiving in return what is necessary for
the satisfaction of his needs; he therefore expressly intends to
acquire a right full and real, not only to the remuneration, but
also to the disposal of such remuneration, just as he pleases.
Thus, if he lives sparingly, saves money, and, for greater secu-
rity, invests his savings in land, the land, in such case, is only
his wages under another form; and, consequently, a working
man's little estate thus purchased should be as completely at
his full disposal as are the wages he receives for his labor."

—POPE LEO XIII[63]

One of the great achievements of Christendom was the ordered, family-centric distribution of land and ownership. Moderns will often harp on feudalism and fancy that
all of those who lived before our so-called freedom were really just slaves of kings just
as they were slaves to the "superstition of religion." We must leave aside that what we
call feudalism was actually an almost endlessly diverse system that does not fit easily in
our caricatures of it. What is most interesting about it, however, is that we still long for

---

63 Leo XIII, Encyclical *Rerum Novarum* (May 15, 1891), no. 5.

the achievements of the medieval lands. We lovingly label our pop-up neighborhoods as such-and-such village, but the village is an invention of Christendom. Modernism has produced efficient housing, but not villages, because villages are from Christian civilization, as John Senior put it: "Anyone caught up in the bad work of real estate development or architecture and building must consider how diligently the atheist has worked, how imaginatively he has constructed housing projects and public buildings to foster his religion; whereas Christians have behind them the best and loveliest housing developments in history in the Catholic villages of Europe, and fail to reproduce them."[64]

The great defender of small farms and a land-based economy Hilaire Belloc claims the danger of our modern economic and industrial direction is precisely in its betrayal of the village. This he shows in *The Servile State,* where he explains that after the fall of Rome, there still existed large holdings of land with populations of servants and slaves to tend them. These were called by the Latin word *villae.* As the centuries moved on, it was the Faith that turned the slaves of the villas leftover from Roman order into stable Christian communities, especially by guaranteeing and guarding their access to productive land. It was through the land and its cultivation, aided by the influence of the Catholic Church, that they were made free. "With every passing generation the ancient servile conception of the labourer's status grows more and more dim," explains Belloc.[65] Eventually, the peasants' ties to the land became enshrined in law and custom, and their eventual achievements of beautiful, ordered, and free villages stemmed most especially because they had full claim, rights, and even ownership of land. It was the Church that turned the servile *villas* into the village, the ideal that we still long for.

Belloc's central thesis of betraying the villages is that industrialization and untethered capitalism will lead inevitably back to slavery. He made the claim that power, once removed from landowning families by and for big businesses, will eventually decay social order in such a way that big businesses will enslave people to their created systems and rob people of the security of land, ownership, and freedom generally. In response to this degradation—again, according to Belloc—governments will seize more control and that will lead to socialism, simply another form of servitude. The people that had

---

64 John Senior, *The Restoration of Christian Culture* (Norfolk, VA: IHS Press, 2008), 64.
65 Hilaire Belloc, *The Servile State* (London: T. N. Foulis, 1913), 47.

once been free on the land will then be tossed to and fro by the powers of big business and big government. Belloc clearly had a point.

Belloc was a part of the English Catholic Land Movement, which advocated that the only way to stop the consolidation of power and money was to keep it distributed as much as possible, not just in the hands of many, but in the hands of *families*. Families, being tied to one another and to their place through homesteading, farming, and craft, would bring back the lively Catholic culture that had been lost.

When revolutionary change disrupts settled peoples, it is often the workers of the land that get displaced and disposed of by the wealthy and powerful. This has happened throughout the history of Christendom, often to the detriment of the local cultures of Catholic villages and regions. This should remind us of the Israelites, who frequently gained, lost, and regained their land as they gained, lost, and regained their freedom and dedication to worshipping God. The dissolution of the monasteries in England, for example, transferred the ownership of lands from monastic holdings to an emerging Protestant aristocracy, which not only often disrupted the economics of villages but also paved the way for religious persecution. Their freedom to work the land was lost during the same time their freedom to right worship was denied. In his various calls for a return to the land in England, Fr. Vincent McNabb would often relate it to the book of Exodus because the purpose of escaping the "city" of Egypt was not just to escape it but to be free to worship God.

After the French Revolution, similarly, there was a desire for an increase in the power and use of banking, which led Catholic advocates like Louis de Bonald to remind their people where true wealth resides. "Morals and laws," he said, were the wealth of nations. And those morals, he argued, were held by communities of families that worked the land. "Everything comes from the land," says Bonald, "just as everything returns to it."[66] Strong families in stable Catholic cultures rooted in actual soil are the truest economic wealth.

This is why the Church, from the very beginning of the industrial era, has been wary of the loss of small holdings of productive land that were worked and loved by families. She was skeptical from the beginning of the transfer and consolidation of ownership

---

66 L. V. de Bonald, *The True and Only Wealth of Nations: Essays on Family, Economy and Society* (Sapientia Press, 2006), 29.

from small communities and families into the hands of the wealthy and powerful. She has been right all along.

This also helps us see that the desire for security in land and freedom from the slavery of the unnatural, money-based economy is reasonable. Catholic homesteaders are not necessarily dismissing all forms and participation in the modern economy, but the increasing immorality of it and its tendency toward excess, artificiality, control, and domination leads us to find a simpler security in owning a bit of land.

SHOULD CHRISTIANS OWN LAND?

Early in the industrial era, the observable destruction of lives and land was not hard to hate. The slums around factories, the pollution, and the deserted homesteads were clearly a degradation of nature and humanity. The cold and calculating cruelty of that time sought the goal of production and profit at any cost.

It was in this environment that people understandably advocated for a more dignified arrangement of the workingman with the massive capital in the hands of the industrialists. The Marxist answer was to empower the people by empowering the government. Marxism has generally proven Belloc correct in that government policies that do not heed the natural need for a family, as Marxism does, will seek to remedy social problems through government control. Bringing order and justice through laws to such a situation is certainly in the power and purpose of the government, but doing so through the Marxist means is usually materialist and often in clear opposition to the order of the natural family. Although there are differences in socialism, communism, and other leftist theories, one of the common tactics of the Marxists was to condemn the few who owned too much and transfer it to the masses through governmental and collective ownership, not private and small ownership.

Christians sometimes had a hard time resisting the call of the Marxists (some still have this trouble). The proposal to take down the mighty, lift up the lowly, and live a life of extreme commonality would naturally appeal to a religion whose Founder recommended as much. The Church's own history, divinely enshrined in her Sacred Scriptures, tells us that her earliest members sold their possessions and held things in common, apparently disburdening themselves of private property in a complete surrender in faith and charity (see Acts 2:44–47). Her religious orders would follow suit, and still do, with varying degrees and arrangements of renounced property. But as Pope Pius XI said, philosophies like socialism, which remove the rights of private property in an attempt to secure the fruit of property, "cannot be reconciled with the teaching of the Catholic Church because its concept of society itself is utterly foreign to Christian truth."[67]

Unlike the Marxists, the Church did not want to see the means of production controlled by the government. Unlike the capitalist,[68] the Church did not want to see the means of production controlled by a few business titans. Because she takes seriously the truth that the family is the cradle and bulwark of society and that a family has more stability and security on the land, she has proposed a wide and diffused distribution of ownership. As to the question of who should be in control of property, business or government, the answer is neither. Rather, it is the family that should be the primary and foundational owner of productive property, especially farmland. It is the family that is most able to draw fruits and culture from the land, not distant owners and investors who hold land as means of profit rather than for direct production.

For many, the hopes of land ownership are distant. However, what we see in the Church's consideration and teaching is that the very purpose of land ownership is that it may bring security and stability to the family as the basis of society. Or, put differently, for the family to be the basis of society, the family benefits greatly from being based on an actual piece of property. This is the first step for many in realizing their hopes for homesteading on a practical level. But as we know, this brings up many more practical issues. Depending on your circumstances, staying where you are might be prudent, but moving may also be necessary. In our hyper-mobile society, this might seem like a small thing. But thinking more deeply and practically about it, we need to recognize the challenges of rooting into a whole new way of life in a whole new place very carefully, which is what we will do in the next chapter.

---

67 Pius XI, Encyclical *Quadragesimo Anno* (May 15, 1931), no. 117.
68 I understand that many readers will take "capitalist" to mean simply "freedom" of the market, but in the Church's eyes, the skepticism of capitalism is in the consolidation of power and the disregard for the laws of God and the good of man for the sake of profit.

Beekeeping for Profit (or Loss) *–Tommy Van Horn*

On a spreadsheet, farming always makes money. The weather is fair, death is never lurking around the corner, and the products always sell. Oh, the folly!

There was a time when I was eager to be farming full-time, so I took to the internet (as any reasonable millennial) for some inspiration and guidance. It worked, sort of. However, I almost crashed our home economy in the process. To those who are churning through ways to make money from the land, be wary if you have little experience and an absence of mentors.

In 2014, three years into our beekeeping and urban farming endeavor, I personally fell into the trap of buying myself into beekeeping. After two years of managing ten to twenty beehives, I figured it was time to scale up, fast. In order to do so, I bought one hundred hives mid-spring in 2014 from a beekeeper who "grows" bees and then sells them. I had my plan on paper and could already see honey by the ton pouring in. Once the bees arrived on the ground via a semi-truck, I divided each colony in half to increase my hive count to 220. It all sounded great, but I made several rookie mistakes that nearly cost me all my bees.

The whole idea came from a YouTube "mentor" who claimed managing two hundred colonies is less than a part-time job of fifteen to twenty hours a week. I learned this could be true if you have decades of experience, an efficient facility, proper equipment, and bees within a proximate location. I failed to factor in the steep learning curve and my proximity (one hour) to the "free" barn I was given on loan to process and store everything. In addition, my various bee yards were spread out over an hour's drive.

The next YouTube mentor told me that when you divide a colony into two, they will always produce their own queen. With this little truth, I was going to double production in no time. The reality is that bees need the proper resources to grow queens and proper hive density to mate virgin queens. Due to poor placement (isolation) and lack of resources in many hives, after I tried to double my production, I learned nearly half the colonies were not bred sufficiently or at all, so many of the colonies ended up in peril.

The lack of experience was debilitating.

Due to a lack of experience, it took me longer to inspect hives since I was timid in culling poor hives.

Due to a lack of experience, I failed to plan for an unexpected drought/dearth and have sufficient supplemental feed on hand and an efficient way to distribute the feed for hives that were light on stored surplus.

Due to lack of experience, I failed to manage my parasitic mite load, and by the end of the season, any colony that did not starve from lack of incoming nectar/food died from being overwhelmed with viruses from the mites.

The following year, at the start of 2015, I was left with thirty-five colonies—down 185 colonies largely due to lack of experience.

I learned a hard lesson: more is not always better; rather, better is always better. Match your capacity to your skill level and success is much more attainable. After that point, I made a promise to not buy bees again but to grow my own bees from my own resources and grow my knowledge and experience in the process, an important but easily overlooked step by the novice. Since that point in 2015, we have turned the thirty-five colonies into seven hundred without buying bees and without skipping steps up the ladder of experience.

I learned the hard way that the goal for a successful (and enjoyable) land-based venture is to match experience, knowledge, and resources. Then from that point, set measurable and attainable goals for the family. A good and honest self-examination with plenty of input from the spouse has since made our return to the land more sustainable and enjoyable.

7

FROM ANYWHERE
TO SOMEWHERE

"Somewhere is better than anywhere."
—FLANNERY O'CONNOR[69]

Moving to homesteading often brings about an actual move. Sometimes that can feel romantic, but it is a grave and serious decision. In fact, one of the principle philosophies that we pick up in modern society is a certain mobility and freedom that may work in opposition to the foundations of homesteading, which is a necessary rootedness. Part of learning to live the liturgy of the land is to relearn the value and necessity of rooting down, which is something worth considering even if we are staying where we are, but especially if we might make a true move to land in a different or rural location.

In his book *Bringing It to the Table,* Wendell Berry checks the zeal of new homesteaders a bit. When most of us speak of owning and working the land with our family, we quickly adopt the name "family farm". But in Berry's definition, one can't simply call any cultivated property a family farm. Given his history within a farming community and his lifelong work advocating for family farms in the specifically American context, his definitions should hold some weight.

First, and most simply, Berry describes what this book has been proposing as a homestead: "What I . . . mean by the term 'family farm' is a farm small enough to be

---

69 Stephen Sparrow, "Getting Somewhere: Baptism and the Sense of Place in Flannery O'Conner's 'The River,'" Comforts of Home (blog), March 4, 2004, https://flanneryoconnor.com/ssbaptism.html.

farmed by a family and one that is farmed by a family, perhaps with a small amount of hired help. I shall not mean a farm that is owned by a family and worked by other people. The family farm is both the home and the workplace of the family that owns it."[70]

His next qualifier is a bit more challenging: "Furthermore, the term 'family farm' implies longevity in the connection between family and farm. A family farm is not a farm that a family has bought on speculation and is only occupying and using until it can be profitably sold. Neither, strictly speaking, is it a farm that a family has newly bought, though, depending on the intentions of the family, we may be able to say that such a farm is potentially a family farm."[71]

As an oak tree is what it is only through time rooted in a place, so too, according to Berry, longevity is what makes a homestead a *tradition and art* and not just an occupation or lifestyle. And humbly acknowledging that Berry is talking to *us the authors*—relatively newcomers to the farm—both of us (Tommy and Jason) have witnessed a startling turnover in new homesteaders, meaning they come with great zeal, perhaps start a blog showing their adventures, put up a [Surname] Farm sign, only to abandon the idea within a couple of years. Obviously, not only do these turnovers likely cause unnecessary strain on the family in the name of bringing peace to it, but it also reveals that there is something within modern man that has a hard time establishing himself in a way that would indeed move toward Berry's idea of the family farm.

AWAY FROM COSMOPOLITANISM

As a man weds his wife in a way that makes him free to love by limiting his love to one woman, so too we are made more free in many ways by dedicating ourselves to the limits of a place. This ideal of rootedness, while sounding romantic to some, is actually one of those aspects of homesteading at odds with much of our societal assumptions and values today. Mark T. Mitchell, the editor of the popular localist publication *Front Porch Republic*, argues the term "cosmopolitan" best describes the modern and liberal ideal of freedom *from* place. He contrasts cosmopolitanism with the mode of living based on *tradition*, which is a limiting and freeing tie to a culture (specific to a place). The cosmopolitan view is the total autonomy of the individual as he relates to his connection

---

70 Wendell Berry, *Bringing It to the Table* (Berkeley, CA: Counterpoint, 2009), 31.
71 Berry, 32.

to other people. For the cosmopolitan, his connection to people is a general embrace of "humanity" and not the limitation of a locale. "The cosmopolitan considers himself a citizen of the world and views other affiliations as secondary to his universal embrace," says Mitchell.[72] Mitchell quotes a "leading contemporary champion" of cosmopolitanism, Martha Nussbaum, as laying out the choice as between the localist, whose allegiance is nearby and tight, and "the person whose primary allegiance is to the community of human beings."[73] Others have said if we tie ourselves too close to a place and its people, we will slow down the progress toward a peaceful global order because men that are too allied to their community "descend into an aggressive and likely violent tribalism."[74]

72 Mark T. Mitchell, *Limits of Liberalism* (Notre Dame, IN: University of Notre Dame Press, 2019), 11.
73 Mitchell, 13.
74 Mitchell, 13.

Against this stands the Catholic Church, which, although she is universal, is not globalist. Catholic means "universal," and Roman means that the universal Church is grounded in a place, Rome. She has gone from that place to other places, respecting and preserving what is good and purifying the bad. By that, we mean that she knows and accepts the God-given order of creation that man lives and operates in a variety of circumstances, and cajoling healthy human variety into a homogenized pattern is what actually produces violence. Since men are prone to love that which they know, we can only know our specific place, and, therefore, when an outside force threatens that place and its people, we defend it. This is perhaps the feared "violent tribalism." Yet, we might note from the sheer facts of history that it is these places that often live in a stable peace, and it is outside forces that, by nature and necessity, are a greater power. In other words, it is the greater power that tends to invade, confiscate, and harm the smaller power.

A local economy, epitomized but not restricted to the local farmer, more naturally creates stability and healthy permanency. The rootedness of a homestead cultivates and sustains true human culture by the fact of its permanence. And it is only when one has a certain rootedness in a place that one can correctly identify a neighbor, which is a word with a very specific and obvious meaning: the people you live close to. The more globalized and abstracted from place an economy becomes, the more the interaction with and need for neighbors diminishes or disappears. This makes the cultivation of true culture and virtue difficult, makes following Our Lord's command to love our neighbor unnecessarily abstract, and can create an unhealthy lack of attachment to our community—the bond that *makes* community.

To avoid the temptation to be transient and disconnected, many religious orders even take a vow of stability, because if each person in a religious community understood themselves and others to be potentially temporary, the relationship is much more like cohabitation—together but uncommitted—which does not lend itself to the bonds that make for human and even religious flourishing.

As it relates to our homesteading, being overly mobile can diminish the knowledge of a place as it relates to the natural world and the peculiarities of a region. Last frost dates, expected rainy seasons, and so on can be looked up online, but this cannot replace the intuitive sense that is gained by experiencing and even growing to love a place by growing things in that place. One also gets to know the people—the mentors, guides, and sages—that can be of real assistance and help when learning the ropes. Talking with the old men at the store about the weather isn't small talk but a big and meaningful communion with others.

This different order and form of community might not happen instantly, and newcomers will need to be patient as they learn to fit in. In many rural places that might have farmers that stretch back generations, there can even be a reasonable skepticism of new homesteaders because so many of them give it a go, fail to integrate with others in their community, and generally reveal themselves to be temporary associates and not lifelong neighbors or friends. Along with short-lived homesteads, there is also a common experience of people buying land for the asset, views, or "space," not a true rootedness for the sake of the people and local culture or economy. Therefore, when settling into a homestead and being open and willing to be a part of that community, one may need to forgo the idea of "plugging in" to a community, which is the modern way we phrase the idea of being socially connected with others. A plug, after all, is something that is inserted into a power source in order to draw something it needs. A plug is a one-way and temporary connection.

Instead of thinking about being "plugged in," again, think about trying to become *rooted* in a place. Roots interconnect with their soil in a way that stabilizes it, becomes a mutually enriching channel for other life, and remains intact for that mutual benefit. As one connects through the natural needs and seasons of homesteading, you will likely be amazed at how natural community starts to grow. A mutually rooted life—one that intertwines practical help and neighborly care—creates a genuinely common good and common life, a culture. It takes patience and time to grow, however. Uprooting such a life can cause harm to both the plant and the surrounding environment. Therefore, to be rooted is to live in such a way that draws and gives life steadily and consistently.

CLOSE OR FAR?

In America, most cities and suburbs are surrounded by rural landscapes within a one- or two-hour drive. Some cities have access to open land within thirty minutes, which makes it possible for a family looking to set roots on a homestead very feasible without having to entirely relocate across the country. Obviously, some things will change when a move is made an hour away, but familiarity with the general vicinity, climate, and culture will make this the easiest point of entry. The other option, although potentially a bit riskier, would be to relocate entirely to a new state or region. Plenty of people have taken this approach, but in addition to learning the homesteading way of life in that place, there will be additional learning curves and the need to discover and cultivate a new community. With any move, there are so many dynamics at play (e.g., income, parish, community, education, climate, family, friends, etc.) that must be addressed as a part of the whole vision for your life and that will help guide the discernment, but either way, the need to send down roots remains.

CONSIDERATIONS FOR A MOVE

We have a more thorough examination in the second section of this book, which covers matters of practical discernment about how your home might be ordered based on your locale and employment, but here are some considerations worth the time for the general idea of relocating.

How Much Land?

If a household is considering a move, the question might come up as to how much land they need. The *Homestead Act* of 1862, for example, defined it as "a lot of land adequate for the maintenance of a family," which was 160 acres at the time. That's a big farm. This is partly because of the sheer land-wealth of North America, with large homesteads being reasonable and attainable. In Wendell Berry's stories and essays, he regularly talks of the eighty-acre, multi-generation farm as a recognized norm[75]—half of that allotted by the original *Homestead Act*. Freed slaves after the Civil War were allotted half of that at forty acres of land in some places, and although it did not continue as a widespread policy, many freed slaves established agrarian communities with plots of about that size. We have experienced regularly that people seem to think twenty acres is what they need—half again of forty acres.

In our experience, twenty acres is way too much land for most, and trying for that might be financially ruinous. You don't need close to that much land to homestead at a decent scale. For the so-called distributists of England, those writers like G. K. Chesterton that proposed a property- and land-based economy rooted in homesteading, the ideal was a phrase repeated in other old-world writings: "three acres and a cow."

---

75 His fictitious examples in the novel *Remembering*, for example, propose and examine literarily the eighty-acre norm, which we know from his other writings is a consideration of real places and farms.

For craftsmen that homestead "on the side," they allotted only an acre for some pigs and a garden. A dear friend of ours who has homesteaded for over twenty years after his "agrarian conversion" raised most of his food on only two acres, focusing on pigs, gardens, a milk cow, and leased land for larger crops like peanuts.

And, of course, there are people who grow quite a bit of food on small suburban plots—sometimes even smaller pieces of soil. When I (Jason) was in grad school, our small but growing family lived in an apartment in Denver, and the neighbor across the street had a decent garden. After a few friendly conversations, he offered me a small plot to grow vegetables about a hundred feet from my front door (which, in an apartment, is the only door).

Community

As to where one ought to move (as in totally new regions), there are places friendlier to homesteading than others in their climate. However, generally, you want to go where you have the most developed sense of the weather and climate, where everything isn't new to you.

But the more urgent question of "where" will be in relation to your life in a community. Some may set out alone, but many more need to consider an existing community. The agrarian life is hard, especially when you are alone, and you need like-minded friends nearby. We must consider, of course, having Catholic families near us that are also homesteading, but there are also many rural places that may be in the country and are devoid of any like-minded people. There are rural communities where there are two groups: industrial farms and impoverished households. The former may not have the time or mindset to offer much help, and the latter is not much different from what you would find in a rough part of an inner city. When considering a piece of property, consider how close you will be to others living a similar life.

Options Other than Owning

For those that do not have the resources to purchase land, there are also many options that can help during the transition, especially if you need to get to know a new place and try your hand at homesteading in the first place. Both of us started out using rented or leased land to live and homestead on, and both of us continue to use leased and rented land for expanded enterprises. There are even forms of leasing that can be more secure than others, but this option should be seriously considered if you simply lack the means to purchase land or if you want to invest more time and money in an actual farm business without tying it all up in land first.

And if you cannot easily purchase land at first, do not think it is necessarily a failure of creativity or hard work. From ancient times to now, it is rare to be able to just arrive on some land and "settle" it, even if that is in our short-term memory as a country due to the style of our Western expansion as a country. Many homesteaders and farmers today have been blessed with inheriting land or having some other financial help in getting to the homestead. This is normal for many but not available to all. Therefore, other creative options—including intergenerational arrangements—can be considered.

From Backyard Bees to Full-Time   *–Tommy Van Horn*

I did not grow up in rural America, but I grew up surrounded by suburban vegetable gardens in the early years of my life (1984–1989). My father worked as a geologist on the Front Range in Colorado, and my mother was a nurse-turned-homemaker when my siblings and I were born. We lived in an average suburban home on an average suburban lot, but most of our backyard was a cultivated garden of raspberries, cherries, herbs, gourds, greens, and maize. Our freezer was typically filled each fall with wild elk, high mountain trout, and the summer surplus from the garden. The realities of seasonality, sacrifice, and solemnity associated with our food were very much a part of my early formative years. At age five, we relocated to Houston, Texas, for my father's work, and with the increased demands of his career and the difficulty of vegetable gardening in the sand and shade of the Piney Woods, we traded cultivators for seasonal flower gardens, fishing poles, and little league sports.

For the remainder of my childhood, sports and school dominated much of my life. However, the natural intuition gained in my early years was still kept alive by assisting my parents with yard work, building "illegal" forts in our community green-belts, and also spending our vacation time each summer camping, fishing, and backpacking in Colorado or in the Appalachian Mountains.

At twenty-six, I was newly married and living in downtown Pensacola, Florida, on a tenth of an acre and was given *Successful Fathers* by James B. Stenson to read. The simple and short book provided a new world view for me: that the home was not historically a place of mere consumption interrupted with housekeeping duties but rather a place of integrated family life, economy, and festivity. Prior to the industrial revolution of the late nineteenth century, the average American home had a necessary family-centric economy that provided natural opportunities for fathers to teach, mentor, and apprentice their children not only in life lessons but in a trade or business venture. However, due to the industrial revolution and a new social policy in place, many families were forced to trade the family farm for a steady paycheck, two weeks of vacation, and a home in town. Reading Stetson's work and reflecting on the impact my own father had on my upbringing and the competency I gained from him in the outdoors, even with the demands of his corporate job, I was inspired to take a similar hands-on approach with our growing family, but in a way that was centered on small business and growing food.

Initially, the vision Emily and I started with was to work toward land-based living as a lifestyle rather than a career because we did not have access to land. I had a steady full-time job working as a director for a nonprofit, and the job was fairly flexible, the work environment was healthy, and I wasn't really looking for a way out. We started a small garden and kept two beehives in our quaint backyard. The following year, we sold the surplus honey to our friends and neighbors, and within days, we were sold out. After looking online and visiting local grocery stores with a marketing eye, it became apparent that there were no local beekeepers marketing their products to our community. Overnight, the passion to tell the story of the bee, beekeeper, and production of honey began to consume my spare time. In 2012, after buying more equipment from a retiring beekeeper and continuing to expand our little cottage business, we decided we needed more space to operate, so we rented our home out to offset our costs and moved down the street in the same neighborhood to rent an older home with a larger yard (half an acre) and a large shed in the backyard, which our friends/landlord graciously assisted us in remodeling into a certified honey house with the proceeds we raised from a crowdfunded Kickstarter campaign.

In addition to the honey house and modest workshop, we also had more space to install a thirty-by-thirty foot kitchen garden in full sun, an eight-hen chicken run, and ten beehives. We were living the dream as urban homesteaders in our old drafty house in Pensacola, Florida. However, in the fall of 2012, I was faced with a dilemma. The honey business had expanded to more than a cottage business, and the demands of my full-time job were requiring more of my attention. At that point, with less than two months' worth of income in savings, we decided to jump full-time into the honey business. We sold our second car and my triathlon bike and plunged headfirst into selling honey. To supplement the production of twenty to thirty hives around town, we aggregated honey from other local beekeepers in fifty-five-gallon drums and packaged and sold the honey at farmers' markets, online, and at local grocery stores. After about six months of dedicated full-time efforts, things really began to take off and the constant concern of paying the bills diminished, slightly. Over the next four years, we continued to operate in the same space and expanded the bees and distribution to the capacity we were capable of. Some years, we saw 30 to 40 percent growth; other years, it was two steps forward and two steps back due to colony collapse disease. Looking back toward the end of our time in Pensacola in 2016, we often laugh at the chaos. Unloading semi-trucks of empty honey bottles in the front yard, moving bees on trucks in the downtown neighborhood, and extracting honey in the honey house literally ten feet from our neighbor's house (luckily we had gracious neighbors who liked honey)! When we got to the point of renting a warehouse thirty minutes from home to store our equipment, extracting honey with our larger system in a friend's empty barn fifty minutes in the other direction, and then storing bulk honey in a third facility, we decided it was time to consolidate and move out of our beloved neighborhood.

We took drives nearly every week in the spring and summer of 2016 looking for an area we could call home. Our prerequisites were:

- The land needed to be an hour or less from Pensacola where we sold our honey weekly and attended the only available Traditional Latin Mass in the area.
- We wanted to be near someone we knew in case of an emergency and for the purpose of community.
- Priced at $150,000 or less. We had built up a modest savings of about $60,000 and borrowed the balance from the Farm Service Agency to purchase the land, establish infrastructure, and build a honey house.
- We wanted five to twenty acres of mostly cleared land. Any improvements (water, power, septic, etc.) were a plus.

We settled on ten acres that were sixty-eight miles from Pensacola in the sleepy timber and agriculture town of Laurel Hill, Florida, for $3,900 per acre. The land was an old peanut farm that had been divided up and parceled out when the previous owner passed away. There were no improvements; however, the price was right, we had two other Catholic families we knew five minutes down the road, and it was on the edge of an hour's commute to Pensacola. The next four years, from 2016 to 2020, were some of the most trying years of my life. We were living in a 168-foot RV for eighteen months with three children and one on the way, self-building a home (with the help of friends, family, and some sub-contractors), and managing the build of our honey house, all the while trying to keep some sense of normalcy with the family, the bees alive, and the honey orders fulfilled. I remember one night before our annual food inspection. The honey house was a disaster, the children were sick, and I was exhausted, nearly breaking down in an anxiety attack (I thought I was having a heart attack at age thirty-three). I was so close to throwing in the towel; the combination of building, business, and family demands pushed me to nearly a breaking point. Thankfully, Emily was always supportive and believed in the dream of homesteading as a family. During that period of 2016–2020, we were honestly not homesteading the

way the pictures in this book depict. We just could not manage additional animals or gardens with small children and our other obligations. Our goal was to establish infrastructure, keep the business going, and wait till our children were more of age to help with animals.

In 2020, we turned a corner. We decided to sell off the retail brand of our business to another beekeeper. This allowed us more time to be on the homestead, focus strictly on bulk honey production, and invest in our homestead. Our oldest daughter was now nine years old and our oldest son was seven—both capable and confident in caring for our cows, rabbits, pigs, and chickens alongside their younger siblings. In 2023, six and a half years after breaking ground in Laurel Hill and thirteen years into the journey from the city to the country, I can say it's starting to feel like a homestead. We have a milk cow that is milked daily, pigs that keep us in pork, chickens that keep us in eggs, a quarter-acre garden, a quarter-acre orchard of various fruits now in their second and third years, and also four to five acres of established pasture for our small flock of hair sheep and black Angus and jersey cows and calves. All this to say, homesteading takes time especially when either time, capital and experience are being slowly acquired.

— 8 —

FROM EXTRACTING
TO CULTIVATING

"The philosophy underlying the use of compost and organic manures generally is the recognition of the order in creation. . . . Human ingenuity may and must intervene in this cycle for the production of food, but man must not allow himself to be carried away by pride. God's infinite intellect measures things; things measure the human intelligence, which can attain to truth only by humbly conforming to them. Man is meant to humbly co-operate with nature, not to seek to dominate it in the spirit of Descartes, or to seek to mold and dictate it, like Marx. Man must respect order and obey nature's rules. Whatever intrusions he makes must be, so to say, in the spirit of these rules; he must on no account flout the underlying principles of natural law nor be in outrageous contradiction to the processes of nature."

—FR. DENIS FAHEY, C.S.SP.[76]

Homesteaders live within the confines and lessons of nature. Although it requires intense use of human agency, homesteading does not lend itself to the delusion that man's work is in full control of anything. The liturgy of the land exists in submission to God's laws, not man-made ones. To homestead, one cannot create reality, as we do in our digitized and technological worlds, but must submit to nature's own needs and life. We are stewards of nature, the highest of the creatures, but we are still not the Creator. To

---

76 Denis Fahey, *The Church and Farming* (Fitzwilliam, NH: Loreto Publications, 2017), 94.

work with it is, in most instances, to submit to it, to tend it toward its own nature, but not to control or dominate it. Part of our conversion to the homestead is rethinking the relationship of man to nature. By submitting to nature's ways, we are submitting to God as Creator.

MAN VS. NATURE

There are dangerous threads in the modern understanding of nature. On the one hand, there are proponents of conserving and protecting nature who treat humans as an essential threat to the earth itself, bringers of destruction, waste, and pollution. To them, humans harm nature by their nature. Therefore, they advocate, for the earth's sake, the limitation of people by a robust encouragement of contraception and abortion—fewer people through murder. Although there certainly must be some truth for us in the caring for natural things, the Catholic is immediately alerted to the evil done in the name of this ideology.

On the other hand, there are those that think our dominion over nature is absolute, that material needs in one place justify the harm done in another, and that we can plunder, kill, and extract from nature whatever we need or simply want. Maybe we plant an extra tree here and there, but generally, we'll be ok because we really need it and technology will likely find a way to fix it anyway later. Accepting the dichotomy of the anti-human nature lovers mentioned above, they put humanity against nature as the thing that must be served above and before the perceived harm done to the earth. After all, are you really going to put the needs of some trees and chipmunks over a human baby?

These should be recognized for what they are: extreme and poorly thought-out positions based more on shallow political pundits and their soundbites than mature reflection on the truth. But, more deeply, these erroneous views represent a deep theological and philosophical error. In developing an understanding of your homestead—and even your community—it is necessary to recognize these extremes as worldly, atheistic, often explicitly evil, and deeply embedded in our thinking. Their grip is so tight on our imagination that we rarely reflect on the harm they may do through us. These errors will need to be overcome in order to have a truly Catholic homestead and to live the liturgy of the land.

GOOD NATURE FROM A GOOD GOD

What the world often means by "nature" are those organic and unmolested places and creatures—plants, animals, soil, lakes, rivers, and oceans. Nature has many parts but is essentially one big material thing that is distinguished and recognized as something *other than man.*

When the Catholic Church uses the term "nature," however, there is an older and more reverent view. Catholics would describe the things of nature—birds, reptiles, shrubs—as *creation.* Man, though part of creation, occupies a different place as being made up of body and soul; he is physical and spiritual at the same time in the same being. And all of creation, in its parts and particulars, has a nature that orients toward the God-given end for which it was created.

The simplest theology of creation comes from Genesis, which we can summarize in three simple points. Developing a coherent and Catholic vision of your homestead requires these truths to remain in view:

1. Creation comes from God.
2. Creation was created *good.*
3. Man is a part of creation but has a unique place as having dominion over it.

This third point—that man has dominion over creation—is the point of distinction where both atheists and even heretics have caused harm to the coherence and order of the truth.

ABSOLUTE DOMINION

We should note that the near worship of nature from environmentalists today has truly jumped into a religious realm that is not only unreasonable but commits the error of diminishing and dismissing the dignity of man in the name of saving nature. But this zeal for the protection of nature is not very old. In fact, it is traceably a response to the side effects of industrialization, the massive rise in pollution from consumerist economies, and the disregard for the integrity and beauty of creation.

Radical environmentalism often takes shape alongside political ideologies associated with secularism and other leftist ideologies, but it did not originate in nature-loving atheists, nor in nature-abusing Christians, but in nature-abusing atheists. Although it is rarely acknowledged by today's secular culture, it was the Enlightenment era atheists that laid the foundation for creation's abuse through a dismissal of God and utilization of the physical sciences. Instead of more people tending the earth humbly and tenderly, our population growth is sustained through increased industrialization, which more readily harms the earth. This led to the subsequent overreaction of some environmentalists we see today.

As they dismissed God from both the physical sciences and the ordering of society, post-Enlightenment thinkers no longer saw creation as brimming with the presence and goodness of God, containing its own order and integrity and, therefore, being something of a "book of God," as St. Bernard put it. No, with God displaced from society, it was *man* that was placed in absolute dominion, and since creation is not only the source of comfort (like food) but also the source of misery and death, it must be put in man's total control. Attitudes shifted, therefore, from working with reverence with a creation entrusted to man by God—behind and within which His presence is known and real— to something to be subdued and controlled for the good of man alone, who is now the supreme being of the universe. In other words, man's *dominion* over nature, which is a gift from God, became man's *domination* of nature, which is the disorder of man's rule. With God's laws out of the way, man was willing to control nature to any extent necessary in order to escape its limits, make more abundant its benefits, and stop it from being the cause of any discomfort.

Benjamin Wiker's book *In Defense of Nature* does a great job of tracing the intellectual framework that atheists built that led to nature's abuse. He traces much of the thought back to Machiavelli, whose brutal pragmatism was willing to do evil things to get what one wanted. He famously spoke of fortune as a female that, if one wanted to have her, one must "hold her down, to beat her and strike her down."[77] Later Enlightenment thinkers, like Francis Bacon, applied these ideas to working with nature by applying the physical sciences in a similarly forceful way. Instead of allowing that man's dominion must humbly work within creation's nature—which comes from God—Bacon insisted that we treat nature as Machiavelli treated fortune, like a reluctant woman not giving us what we want without force. He wanted a totally "new examination of nature" that acknowledged that nature produces and gives "much more . . . under constraint and vexed; that is to say, when by art and the hands of man she is forced out of her natural state, and squeezed and moulded. . . . [For] the nature of things betrays

---

77 Benjamin Wiker, *In Defense of Nature* (Steubenville, OH: Emmaus Road Publishing, 2017), 15.

itself more readily under the vexations of art than in its natural freedom."[78] A student of Bacon, Rene Descartes, who is known as a father of our modern secular sciences, said that the goal of science was to "make ourselves . . . masters and possessors of nature."[79] Catholicism does not propose that man's dominion is exercised in this spirit.

In Joseph Ratzinger's book *In the Beginning*, he comes to the defense of the Church to those that think it was Christianity that produced the destructive tendencies of man because of the command of God to subdue the earth. Along with showing how this is a total misunderstanding of the stewardship of the land clearly communicated in Sacred Scripture, he also reminds us that it was modern thinkers, especially of the Marxist sort, that paved the way for natural destruction precisely because they concerned themselves with man alone without reference to God:

> [Marx] was the one who said that humankind should no longer in-quire into its origins and that to do so would be to act foolishly. Marx's intentions here was to move from the question of understanding the "whence" of the universe and its design . . . since creation in its inner-most reasonableness attested most strongly and ineluctably to the Cre-ator, from whom we can never emancipate ourselves. Inasmuch as the question of creation can ultimately not be answered apart from creating Intelligence, the question is seen as foolish from the very start. Creation is of no consequence; it is humanity that must produce the real cre-ation, and it is that which will count for something. This is the source of the change in humanity's fundamental directive vis-à-vis the world; it was at this point that progress became the real truth and matter became the material out of which human beings would create a world that was worth being lived in.[80]

Romano Guardini notes the connection between our domination of nature and our distance from it. "We have both withdrawn from nature and mastered it," he says, which helps us see that, as we dominate the world by violence, we also remove ourselves

---

78 Wiker, 17.

79 Wiker, 11.

80 Joseph Ratzinger, *'In the Beginning...' A Catholic Understanding of the Story of Creation and the Fall* (Grand Rapids, MI: William B. Eerdmans Publishing Company), 35–36.

from it.[81] Part of the life of the Catholic homestead is drawing closer to nature as stewarding sons of God, not masters of control and production. The importance of retuning ourselves to nature is that it will not only help our homesteads be more fruitful but also allow us to witness to the truth. As conservationists like Wendell Berry and Aldo Leopold have advocated, we need a truly conservative approach to conservation, which conserves that which has value, which includes human presence and culture. It is also rooted in being God's stewards: "By creating, God called into being from nothing all that began to exist outside himself. But God's creative act does not end here. What comes forth from nothing would return to nothing if it were left to itself and not conserved in being by the Creator. Having created the cosmos, God continues to create it, by maintaining it in existence. Conservation is a continuous creation (*conservatio est continua creatio*)."[82]

This is why true conservatism and conservation must have an agrarian element, because we are healing our union with nature, not just drawing a line between man and the earth. The Catholic homestead ought to be a place that shows we can till and keep the garden at the same time. In fact, it is our working of the land that strikes what we might call the right balance because work is the relationship of man to the earth, the means of connection. Genesis 2:5, for example, speaks of a deficiency in the land because man had not come yet, there was "no man to till the ground."

Living the liturgy of the land simply cannot see itself at war with nature in this way, in a zero-sum game of power.

MAKING PEACE, NOT WAR

Although man's place as steward and "lord" of creation is meant to be of peaceful cultivation, let's not forget that there is good reason to feel like man is at war with nature. Fire burns and thorns pierce. But Catholics know this is a defect not in nature but in man. Cardinal Stefan Wyszynski reminds us that this is not a defect in the Creator's wisdom or goodness but that it comes from sin: "The fatigue of work also arises out of the fact that, from the very moment of the original sin of Adam, there has prevailed in the world a revolt of nature against man. Matter answers revolt with revolt. Man refused

---

81 Romano Guardini, *Letters from Lake Cuomo: Explorations in Technology and the Human Race* (Grand Rapids, MI: William B. Eerdmans, 1994), 21.
82 John Paul II, General Audience (May 7, 1986), https://inters.org/John-Paul-II-Catechesis-Providence-Care.

allegiance to God, and, infected by this bad example, the created world stiffened in opposition to man."[83]

But, he points out, creation still wants the return of its lord, which is man, designated by God for this task. "From the moment when the king of creatures lost his crown of grace, the world has only been subject to him under protest. 'The whole of nature, as we know, groans in a common travail all the while.'"[84]

For the homesteader, there will be times when it feels like your land is rebelling against you. But in deference to the Creator, we more readily want to work within nature's ways as closely as possible. The thorns we experience are reminders of our sins and calls to peaceful cultivation. There are times when our dominion takes more control, but this must be done more with fatherly care than as a tyrant, meaning we use our dominion in a way that ultimately brings healing and growth, not just subjection. As earthly fatherhood takes its name from God, who is a Father (see Eph 3:14), so too our husbandry should take its name from God, who is a farmer (see Jn 15:1).

Very often, when a problem arises, there are two directions a man's mind can go. In one direction is the technical or mechanical approach, which is often more controlling and artificial. Machines come in part from the genius of man, yet without reverence toward God and the created nature of your homestead, confidence in machines and the application of technical or chemical methods may bring your land into subjection, but it is very often to the detriment of its created nature. In the other direction is the tending and augmenting of the natural processes within nature itself. Natural methods tend to be slower, sometimes more laborious, but in the end, they tend to bring a greater fruitfulness to that which you are tending.

It is wrong to think simply in terms of either/or. People often limit their understanding of the use of mechanical and artificial means in this way, but observers from Hilaire Belloc to E. F. Schumacher have proposed that someone who has an affection for their land through a bond to it—that is, a family or small producer—is more likely to use them wisely than a distant owner extracting profit. Remember, Our Lord said that it is the hired man that runs off when things go bad for his flock, but the man who owns and cares tends to see it through in virtue.

---

83 Stefan Cardinal Wyszynki, *All You who Labor: Work and the Sanctification of Daily Life* (Manchester, NH: Sophia Institute Press), 89.
84 Wyszynki, 89. He is quoting St. Paul in Romans 8:22.

Let's take the garden for example. New seeds benefit from being planted in loose, well-drained, and fertile soil with little competition from other plants. Therefore, it is not uncommon to use a tiller, which turns the soil, breaks up clumps, integrates organic material, increases drainage, and decreases competition from other plants, like grass, by turning them under. But in the name of increasing yield, it can also diminish fertility if not done with care. Although there can be times to work the soil, overdoing it can disrupt millions of living things that, when thriving and left alone, naturally bring fertility to the soil. These are things like worms, bacteria, and the natural process of decomposition that is always occurring in healthy soil. When these things diminish in regularly tilled soils, the application of synthetic and artificial fertilizers may become necessary for the plants to get the nutrients they need to be fruitful. A side effect of these fertilizers is that, over time, they can decrease natural fertility, and therefore, your soil becomes somewhat addicted to an ever-increasing need for them. Tilling and fertilizing lead to more tilling and fertilizing. The Dust Bowl is a great example of tilling applied too liberally and the land losing its fertility. The farmers found themselves unable to keep up with the desert they created by working the soil, and they also

couldn't afford the fertilizer and equipment that would have been needed to extract a crop from the abused soil.

The process of tilling also gets rid of weeds for a time, but soil is very modest and hates to be bare, so she immediately germinates as many weeds as possible to cover up. Without control, these weeds can completely consume a garden. It is possible that the exacerbated homesteader, who used the tiller in the first place that created the explosion of weeds, and who wants so badly to see his labor's fruits, must appeal again to an artificial and potentially problematic means of over-tilling or even chemicals—poisons. Using poison to grow food is a contradiction we should want to avoid. Even just tilling in such a way that nutrients flow away with the rain is a grave mistake, as one priest humorously put it: "Plowing straight up and down the hills is like stabbing into the back of the soil. I told farmers they would receive absolution for any sin they confessed, but God help them if they confessed plowing straight up and down the hills."[85]

We can see in this example the real benefits, like speed, through the intensification of man's strength, but there are some real downsides. In the first place, it costs money,

---

85 I found this quote in Michael J. Woods, *Cultivating Soil and Soul: Twentieth-Century Catholic Agrarians Embrace the Liturgical Movement* (Collegeville, MN: Liturgical Press), xvii. To anyone who doesn't get it, the priest is not literally denying absolution but communicating the gravity of harming the land.

so it creates a need to engage in the artificial economy by outside purchases instead of appealing to and harnessing natural processes. Next, when a mechanical or industrial approach is applied, it often begets the need for more of these types of solutions. Oftentimes, when we start down this road and encounter problems, our thoughts tend toward solutions by purchasing the next product—"what do I need to spray to fix this problem?" Therefore, the farm controlled and worked by machines can actually become more expensive and, ironically, less fertile. In other words, when we diminish fertility through work, we till and *lose* the garden instead of tilling and keeping it.

The natural approach to the garden is very different. If one does till and work the soil, there must be an understanding of this as a sort of wounding that can be healed. In such a case, we think of it more like *discipline*, which can cause pain, but like God who wounds but heals through His fatherly discipline, we will need to be attentive as we follow up tilling with healing.

One would, for example, note that the forests do not have weeds and steadily increase in life and fruitfulness without inputs. This is because the trees mulch themselves annually in the fall, and this gift of leaves to the soil not only does away with the need for the soil to sprout weeds through mulching (though the seeds are there in the soil should the need arise), but the decomposition increases the fertility around the tree. The trees and the soil work together to feed each other, and within these natural systems, there is a steady increase in fruitfulness. Mimicking such logic, the more natural approach relies heavily on compost. Composting is the process whereby nature puts to death the old and brings the resurrection of new life. It is slower than synthetic fertilizers, but it not only feeds the plants what they need but also, if applied generously to the soil, can act as a mulch, removing the need for weeds to sprout, because the modesty of the soil is never disrupted. Although there may be times to till it in, it is much more effective to consistently apply it to the top of the soil and let the natural processes of creation work it in. Over time, worms are attracted by the compost and create little highways in the soil that beneficial life—bacteria and fungi, for example—make use of.

The natural approach is slower. It also uses those things that are cheap or free. Its primary fruitfulness is in the work applied by man to help along or augment the natural processes. Ultimately, however, it represents and manifests the truth that working within nature's ways creates more fertility, not less. The logic of the seed—that a little work makes fruitfulness without diminishing life—is present.

MAN BUILDS ON NATURE

There is a well-known saying in theology that grace builds on nature. The meaning gets translated in various ways, often in erroneous ways—perhaps because of the word "builds." What is being communicated is that God's action in our lives does not supplant or destroy what is in us naturally. Our nature, after all, is created by God. God, who indeed makes us a new creation by grace, does not, therefore, repudiate what is truly natural in us; it is a nature that comes *from* Him. The more precise meaning is seen more clearly in Saint Thomas Aquinas's phrase: "Gratia non tollit naturam, sed perficit."[86] We would say more truly that grace—God's work in us—does not harm our nature but brings it to perfection (*sed perfecit*). There is nothing translated as "build" in the phrase, but the sense is that God's grace acts in us more like a farmer, giving life, and not something replacing or destroying what is truly natural in us. God's grace can be violent to our sin, ego, and habits, but not toward our created nature.

An acorn, for example, can become an oak tree, but not without the gift of rain, soil, and sunshine. So too man can become mature, even a saint, by the help of grace. When this happens, the "acorn" of man doesn't become something different but rather something in keeping with its nature and purpose.

Made in God's image and likeness and commanded explicitly to "till and keep" as an extension of our connection to the Creator, which is higher than the beasts yet submitted to God's ways and laws, we too want to work with land and animals in ways that do not destroy nature but work it toward greater perfection. Before the Fall, there was harmony between man in his relationship with God, nature, others, and even himself. Grace brings these things back into right order and right relationship. The perfection of our nature, which brings it to an abundant and flourishing fruitfulness, would be impossible without Him. A Catholic homesteader does the same with his land. To be clear, the work of man does indeed alter or change the state of a natural place from what it would be without us, yet it is also true that the work we do should not destroy but bring what is already good to greater perfection. We are not absolute conservationists that think nature is only good when left alone. If that were true, Adam was violating this law when he fulfilled God's command to till and keep. The key is, we want to till *and* keep, to preserve what is true and good—and even beautiful—in nature as

---

86 *Summa Theologica*, I-II, a. 8, q. 2.

we work. As it is the glory of man to live in God, so too nature itself can be tended by man to greater glory, not less. "This work alters, to be sure," says R. J. Snell, speaking of the need for man to both work and preserve the soil, "but an alteration actualizing the earth's own potentiality."[87]

Our actions toward and care for our fellow creatures help us to see and honor the God who is behind them all. Many agrarian authors have noted that the rise in abuse of people often goes alongside abuse of the lower parts of creation, especially land and animals. Aquinas notes this connection when he says the brutal slaughtering of animals was forbidden in the old law "because this form of death is very painful to the victim; and the Lord wished to withdraw them from cruelty even in regard to irrational animals, so as to be less inclined to be cruel to other men, through being used to be kind to beasts."[88]

Therefore, learning to see our land and domesticated animals not as something that can be extracted from without care but as having their own nature is critical to developing an eye to really see what you should do—and not do.

Some erroneously dismiss natural methods as part of faddish environmentalism. Others disdain it as impractical, which is ironically the same argument used against the Church's social teaching on everything from contraception to economics. Once again, however, there are theological implications behind our actions.

Learning to homestead in this way will take time to get to know your land and its inner logic. Jared Staudt argues in *Restoring Humanity* that it is the consistent definition of truth by Saint Thomas Aquinas that helps us to see that the *practicality* of anything requires *knowledge and perception of truth*. But as we saw above, the post-Enlightenment atheists paved the way for utilizing truth by force and effort, not first by contemplating and accepting the truth. "St. Thomas relates that 'truth is defined by conformity of intellect to thing,'" explains Staudt.[89] But in our modernist age, accepting this simple definition can no longer be taken for granted. Truth does not arise in human creation or assertion; it is not an agenda to force on others. It arises from perception of what is and the conformity of the mind to this reality. . . . Understanding the nature of something leads further to the knowledge of what to do with this knowledge

---

87 R. J. Snell, *Acedia and Its Discontents: Metaphysical Boredom in an Empire of Desire* (Kattering, OH: Angelico Press, 2015), 41.
88 *Summa Theologica*, I-II, a. 102, q. 6.
89 Jared Staudt, *Restoring Humanity* (Belmont, NC: Divine Providence Press, 2020), 110.

or to do in response to it in practical wisdom. There is the truth of knowing what is good to do (practical truth). In order to know what is good for human action, it is necessary to know what kind of things human beings are (a speculative truth) and what actions lead to the attainment of the end or goal of human life (a practical truth).[90]

Homesteading is also not an agenda that can be forced on nature. Homesteading especially, because it is so close to the natural forces of creation, has an even greater and practical need to conform to the truth. Not doing so not only damages living things but can lead to the loss of necessary things, such as food. As we see in the example of the garden, not only can working within this truth be an act of faith in its submission to the natural laws given by God, but it also *increases* the fertility of nature. As the trees and the soil work to feed and care for each other, our working within and alongside creation is a mutually enriching benefit. We are not in essence at war with nature. Though sin makes it seem so at times, we want to make peace with nature because it is a gift from God.

90 Staudt, 110.

9

FROM CONTROLLING SCARCITY TO GENEROUS ABUNDANCE

"For the soil which is tilled and cultivated with toil and skill utterly changes its condition; it was wild before, now it is fruitful; was barren, but now brings forth in abundance. That which has thus altered and improved the land becomes so truly part of itself as to be in great measure indistinguishable and inseparable from it."

—POPE LEO XIII[91]

Along with an abusive tendency to extract from nature whatever one desires, there is a related attitude toward creation, one that comes when man's interests are pitted against the earth's, that says the earth is a place of *scarcity*. To some, the natural resources of creation are not only limited but diminishing. They must be gathered and protected before they're gone. The law of charity, which is to love God and love our neighbor, is something that doesn't seem to be within this consideration of how the earth is or isn't fruitful. But it very much is. Unlike industrialized creations, God's creation is conceived in love; charity is the order and foundation of nature. How we understand the goods of the earth—how they come about and what our responsibility with them is—very much shapes how we view our neighbor, especially regarding the spirit of generosity and abundance that is so embedded in our theology.

---

91 Leo XIII, Encyclical *Rerum Novarum* (May 15, 1891), no. 10.

If a disposition that sees creation as scarce mixes with an economic attitude that thinks the order of our work is to outdo and out-compete our neighbor, it will be hard not to slip into a competitive enmity with our neighbor. Not only are we jealous for our own goods, but we are envious of the goods of others. If the primary goods we seek are finite, and if there is an increasing population of men, then competitive hoarding is more reasonable and maybe necessary. As much as caring for our neighbor sounds nice, one must simply look out for his own from the necessity of survival and self-preservation. Although we try to keep it peaceable, our relationships with each other—and even between nations—are necessarily *competitive* since survival belongs to the fittest, which means those who get and keep more of the limited goods. Neighbors are good and all until their presence is such that for them to increase, I must decrease, which means I have to make sure that I increase before they do.

Like the issue of abusing land to get its goods, so too this disposition is a theological problem. For example, if one proposes that the world is overpopulated and therefore must have its population limited or even destroyed, this presupposes that God made the earth in such a way that it cannot support man through man's cultivation and harvesting of the world's fruits. If the earth is scarce, then God either missed a glaring defect in His creation or He is not a loving Father that provides for His children.

Or do we have it all wrong?

What a homesteader learns as he experiences the goodness and fruitfulness of nature is that the world is indeed abundant. The reason we can trust God is that He does care for us, and not only are we allowed to feel that goodness through nature's abundance, but that is also the primary place we come to know directly God's care for us. We know that God's care is not disconnected from our physical nature, but often works through and alongside it. Therefore, although we know there are times when He miraculously feeds us—as the manna in the desert or Christ's feeding of the five thousand shows us—He provides for us and our bodily needs through created nature. Something does not need to be miraculous to be from God, as all things are from Him. We proclaim this through our daily prayers before meals when we call the food "Thy [God's] gifts which we are about to receive from Thy *bounty*." From God, we receive food bountifully. Because they truly are His, we are prepared to share them with our brothers.

There are ways, however, that the abundance of creation can be diminished to the point of scarcity, primarily through sin and carelessness.

WHOSE ABUNDANCE?

First, in our modern mindsets, we often misunderstand what the Church calls the universal destination of goods, which refers to the fact that what is cultivated and tended in creation cannot be hoarded in absolute ownership by some at the expense of others. This often grates on our modern individualism because we see it as acceptable to hold on to goods under no other banner than private ownership. Perhaps you have read of the episode experienced by the Wilder family in *The Long Winter* (one of the "little house" books so often faulted for inspiring families to start homesteading). Due to an extreme winter storm, a town is buried in snow and running out of food. Some remember there is a farmer outside of town that had a good crop of grain. So Almanzo, a son of a farmer, goes out in the perilous weather to find him. The journey is so cold and dangerous that many expect his death. Amazingly, he finds the farmer even though the world is blinded by the ongoing blizzard. The farmer then hears of the town's need, of hungry families. He is sympathetic but also a bit critical of those that failed to prepare well enough. Yet, he refuses to part with the grain. It isn't that he merely doesn't want to give it away. He won't even sell it to Almanzo. His reason is simple. It is his and he wants to use it for seed to make more grain for a greater return on his work from what he owns by right.

The Church's traditional teaching defends the rights of man to own and store his natural wealth. But in the natural and virtuous economy, the *purpose* of wealth is never for profit but is always directed toward some end, always *for* something—for people. This is part of nature itself, since by ownership, man produces stability in the care for himself and his family. Yet, creation was not given by God to man as pre-divided properties but as a common home and gift. It is by man's working that nature is divided into properties and varying arrangements of ownership, but in the beginning and at the end of time, this ownership no longer holds. Ownership is finite, even temporary, which is why it is much more fitting to call it stewardship, a word used by Catholics because we acknowledge all things ultimately belong to God. Ownership is defensible but artificial in the strictest sense. Therefore, there are times when the social construct of ownership gives way to the higher rights of God over His own creation, and if He chooses and directs the sacrifice of goods for the good of another, this is no evil, because man's stewardship over creation is not absolute; God's is. As a good father expects his children to share the gifts that he has given, so too God makes explicit His expectation and even command that we care

for one another's bodily needs. For the farmer to not give the grain shows not just a lack of generosity but a spirit of greed and even mistrust of God's care.

Saint Thomas Aquinas explains that "the temporal goods which God grants us, are ours as to the ownership, but as to the use of them, they belong not to us alone but also to such others as we are able to succor out of what we have over and above our needs."[92] Therefore, God intends to care for man through man's labor, which allows for the ownership of goods, but God also cares for us through the generosity of others. God, therefore, inspires us to generosity, but vices like avarice and greed dissuade us from sharing these goods. A lack of generosity is more easily felt in artificial ownership, like money, but the abundance of creation often gives way to a higher way of generosity.

Not only does the rich man who fails to share with the poor endanger his own salvation ("some are punished eternally for omitting to give alms," says Aquinas in reference to the parable of Lazarus[93]), but he proposes to the poor and the world that the very order of creation is one of scarcity—there isn't enough for everyone—and therefore contributes to a lack of trust in the goodness of God. Thus, a rich man that is not generous with his goods can conceal or distort God's image because he shows that one with power and wealth (which God certainly has) is not benevolent and generous (which God is).

The homestead not only provides the lesson that creation is abundant and we are, therefore, safe to be generous. It also provides many practical opportunities to be generous. Anyone with some tomatoes and squash in the garden knows that the abundance overwhelms the needs of a home quickly. Since those goods are finite and temporary, we feel compelled to find a way to feed someone with them. The lesson of the tomato can be writ large in reminding us that all goods are in fact finite and temporary and that by being faithful and generous stewards of them, we truly store up the higher goods of them in heaven when we give them away.

CARELESSNESS

But there is another way related to nature itself that the world *can* become scarce, and that is through the misuse of land. Fertility is natural to the soil, but it is something that, like many things, takes a long time to build but a short time to destroy.

---

92 *Summa Theologica*, II-II, q. 32, a. 5, ad. 2.
93 *Summa Theologica*, II-II, q. 32, a. 5, SC.

One of the amazing things about man's ability to work with nature is that we increase its fruitfulness through our work. We often think of work only in its somewhat destructive sense, like cutting down a tree for lumber. But with care and attention, our use of the land for the life of man does not have to diminish its fruitfulness as a whole. As we have been proposing throughout this book, when done in accord with nature's laws, our work can increase fruitfulness. Our Lord even borrows this truth to show how God, when He works in us, brings greater fruitfulness even as He works in ways that might hurt. For example, Our Lord relates God the Father to a vinedresser who prunes us in order to make us more fruitful. Many farmers know that the act of pruning indeed

does make a vine more fruitful because grapes only grow on new wood, wood that grows in response to pruning. In the case of harvesting lumber, there are many methods of forestry besides clearcutting wherein certain trees are left and others harvested that lead to an increasing presence of good trees *and* good potential lumber. In places where there are no longer vast forests that can be cut, like in North America, there have been methods honed over the years that leave good and diverse trees in a forest and take out the lesser trees, leaving the best. This is the opposite of clearcutting, which takes the best and leaves the worst and replants vast numbers of a single species for the sake of easier and cheaper harvesting. More sustainable forestry can take a reasonable amount that increases the overall health of the forest *and* supplies the needs of man.

But fertility can be raked away very quickly. Mechanical and technological advances have made working the soil as simple as turning the key on a tractor. Yet, there is danger in the ease of the work. It can lead more easily to hubris or carelessness. Industrialized agriculture has tended by nature to simplification in order to increase productivity and profit. Part of it is also the industrial modeling of inputs and outputs, as opposed to cultivation and tending. The purpose of anything that is industrialized is ultimately for profit and production, whereas on the Catholic homestead, there is the greater call to cultivate virtue, which works alongside the practical need for the fruits of the earth and the work it requires to receive them. The use of chemical fertilizers has replaced more natural methods of soil building, and this has depleted our continent's overall soil health tremendously. Therefore, farming creates scarcity by depleting fertility in the name of growing more food. There are ways we can abuse the soil that actually turn a fertile place into a literal desert. In fact, the history of the Dust Bowl, which was caused by overworking the soil and a rapid increase of mechanized farming, happened in a matter of years due to careless and even violent application of industrialism to the soil. Not only did the depleted land not grow much food, but it displaced thousands of families who were no longer sustained there.[94]

---

94 I would be remiss not to note that there are many very good farmers that make use of artificial fertilizers and machines. However, the slow and steady change of farming toward this model has in many ways forced this reality on them, and they maintain it not from considered wisdom handed on but as a situation inherited but not of their own making. There can clearly be differing degrees of carelessness, and there are certainly an increasing number of farmers more careful than others in the use of machines and chemicals, but it is nonetheless true that small holdings cultivated with greater variety and care represent a wholly other order of farming that should be extolled.

A Toast to the Finest Brewers in the World   *–Tommy Van Horn*

Working in various forms of entrepreneurship over the last fifteen years in the American landscape, the messages that dominate the headlines, books, and success stories are largely about finding your passion, or the next product that can make you wealthy or liberate you from work. There are plenty of products and services today that provide little to no value to society, but thankfully, they tend to fizzle in time unless they have a limitless amount of marketing dollars to keep the facade propped up.

But this idea of amassing wealth that is advertised has always been one I've wrestled with. We need money in a cash-based society to exchange goods and services. It's a means. I get it. But it's the question of what is enough and to what end that has always pinged around in my mind. On one hand, we see Our Lord, who we are called to emulate, live a life of extreme poverty and instruct His followers: "Blessed are the poor in spirit, for theirs is the kingdom of heaven" (Mt 5:3). "If you would be perfect, go, sell what you have, give it to the poor and come, follow me" (Mt 19:21). "So therefore, whoever of you does not renounce all that he has cannot be my disciple" (Lk 14:33). In addition, the vast majority of saints who the Church has elevated over the centuries also embraced poverty and detachment from earthly possessions. Saint Anthony Mary Claret, confessor to the queen of Spain and archbishop of Santiago de Cuba in the 1800s "had nothing, wanted nothing, refused everything. [He] was content with the clothes [he] had on and the food that was set before [him]. [He] carried all [he] had in a bandanna. The contents of [his] luggage were a full-year breviary, a sheaf of sermons, a pair of socks, and an extra shirt—nothing more."[95]

On the other hand, we argue that laymen of the twenty-first century have different material responsibilities and needs than a celibate priest of the later nineteenth century, right? We are called to be fruitful and multiply and protect and provide the necessities of life for our family, but to what degree? Do my children need smartphones, trendy clothing, and a bedroom of their own? Am I depriving them or myself of moral goods by not giving them every opportunity society declares to be good? It seems prudence must be used in many of the hazy areas as each family situation has some nuance to it, but as Catholic fathers, should our end not be the same?

In sharing my intellectual wrestling on work, wealth, and family life, a good friend of mine invited our family over to his house for a burger and beer brewing event. I

---

95 *The Autobiography of St Anthony Mary Claret*, ed. Jose Maria Vinas (Chicago: Claretian Publications, 1976), 65.

am not a brewer nor a beer connoisseur by any means, but I can certainly appreciate a good beer. As the mash was set to boil, he went inside and came out with two chilled beers, both devoid of a label other than the inscription of "XII" on the cap.

Apparently, the beer came across the pond from the Belgium Trappist monks of Westvleteren. The beer was good, but upon learning more (and consuming more of the 10.2 percent ABV), the story only got better. These monks produce, year after year, the highest-rated beer worldwide by beer connoisseurs. What got my attention, though, was that the monks literally only brewed enough beer to cover their expenses, and then they would stop. This is something unthinkable by the modern entrepreneur—to have the highest-rated product in the world and only sell enough to cover your needs; they must be madmen! It turns American capitalism (and, for that matter, all the other economic -isms) on its head and orients the end of the business venture arguably to its proper end. Father Abbott is quoted frequently when pressed to increase production: "We are not monks who brew beer. We brew beer to afford being monks."[96] It seems to me that this orientation of placing profit as a servant to their life as monks in prayer and contemplation is a model for even the layman today. While we may not have the same quantity of time each day to dedicate to prayer as a monk, we can still "inscribe this first law of Christian economics on our hearts [that] the purpose of work is not profit—but prayer."

---

96 Stephen Castle, "Monks who make world's best beer pray for quiet life," *The Independent*, August 10, 2005, https://www.independent.co.uk/news/world/europe/monks-who-make-world-s-best-beer-pray-for-quiet -life-5347131.html.

AGAINST SLOTH

In considering the earth as abundant alongside our obligation to be generous, we cannot help but consider the damaging vice of sloth—laziness. One might be reasonably skeptical of those who are not humble receivers of a generous giver but what we might call moochers. What is interesting about this point is that Sacred Scripture relates the damage that laziness can bring about precisely in these two areas we have discussed: in not working with creation and in working carelessly with it.

LET THE LAZY BE HUNGRY

First, as to our work's connection to eating, it is clear that the lazy should be punished—feel the weight of their sloth—in the place of work's primary purpose: food. "If any one will not work," says Saint Paul, "let him not eat" (2 Thes 3:10). Laziness is shameful, he says elsewhere, because of its bad example to the community and because it makes you dependent on them: "Work with your hands, as we charge you; so that you may command the respect of outsiders, and be dependent on nobody" (1 Thes 4:11–12). The generosity of man should be an occasion not of disordered dependence but of humbly receiving and seeing true needs. In a modern setting, when so much time and money is spent on superfluous and luxurious things, it can be hard to know in what way we ought to be generous. How much jewelry should be shared with the unadorned? Yet, in the realm of food and the work that brings it forth, there is a simpler and holier connection to the natural order of work, gift, and generosity.

The call to be generous balances with the call to work because all true work of man is work for the common good, never solely for a private good. It is the virtue of prudence that "considers things afar off in so far as they tend to be a help or a hindrance to that which has to be done at the present time."[97] Our work is often directed, therefore, by current and future needs that are first for ourselves and our homes. Yet, Aquinas also checks us if that prudent self-preservation becomes too individually focused: "The individual good is impossible without the common good of the family, state, or kingdom."[98] Catholic homesteads not only start back at the simplicity of providing food for our family but as networks of them grow, they ought to move outward in their generosity, from household to community to country, as we have it in our present times.

---

97 *Summa Theologica*, II-II, q. 47, art. 10.
98 *Summa Theologica*, II-II, q. 47, art. 10.

PROTECT THE LAND FROM THE LAZY

The second form of laziness condemned in Scripture is what we have been calling the careless farmer: one who destroys the land by his work or lack of it. Proverbs bemoans the vineyards where idleness reigns, where weeds and thorns grow from neglect (see Prv 24:30–34). The reason this too is considered within the realm of the common good is that it also shows how our work is a social issue. The careless farmer diminishes the fruitfulness of the earth, and to diminish fertility is to take potential food away from our community and even our own progeny. This is where we might note that a more traditional reading of the word "sloth" includes the sin of acedia, which is not necessarily or only inaction but can even mean busyness. On the farm, sloth can be a kind of rushing that harms the land *or* neglects it.

The Catholic homestead, being oriented toward our true end, which is God, is a beacon of hope against the despairing state of both sin and the abuse of the land. The Catholic homestead operates more in the natural economy and, trusting in God, both prepares with rigorous work and shares these goods with great generosity. It does this by being careful with the land in its care, tending it as God tends us, with necessary work that is fruitful for both the worker and the land being worked. Also, since a homestead necessarily does away with the superfluous and luxurious, the simplicity of life is reoriented back to appreciating the abundance of the land itself as the most enjoyable and spiritually safe act. It is an observable phenomenon that those that live close to the land, in simplicity and even poverty, have a greater sense of gratitude for the abundance of life than those that have more security in material goods and money. The homesteader's limitations of material goods and enjoyment of natural goods not only cast off spiritually dangerous superfluities but prepare us to be generous with the abundance that we more easily recognize as coming from God.

OPEN TO RISK

Returning to the error of the earth's limitations, Catholic homesteaders do well to connect an attitude in the scarce earth alarmists with those that would deride large families as irresponsible and risky. In other words, there's a connection between how we see the earth's fertility and how we see our own family's fertility. We're told by God that, along with tilling and keeping, we are to be fruitful and multiply, but the world seems to not believe that multiplication is indeed fruitful. This is no slight or light difference. If love is as God says it is, and the world truly was created from love Himself, then the mutual gift of love is fruitful. Fruitfulness is the way of creation because it is the way of love.

John Senior connected these dots in *The Death of Christian Culture*. There is a connection with seeing creation as something that grows by love, not just depletes. There is a connection in believing that love truly does plant seeds that grow into more goodness, not just take it away. Experts "said two hundred years ago that population growth would outrun the food supply in England by 1850," says Senior. "He was wildly wrong."[99] Others applied scientific agriculture at the promptings of the Zero Population Group to India, and the result was "socialism and hybrid grain."[100] Today, there is a disastrous track record of Western ideologues trying to compel Africans to limit and avoid their own fertility and harness the power of industrial agriculture. The result, like India's, has been the loss of culture and fertility and greater dependence on a more globalist and secular economic order. There is a consistent connection between controlling government programs, industrialized agriculture, and a disdain for the natural fertility of the family. John Senior says:

> They say a finite planet cannot sustain an infinite increase of population. Earth, they say, is like a space ship with limited life supports. But man is part of earth and not merely on it. . . . Increase and multiply—

---

99 John Senior, *The Death of Christian Culture* (Norfolk, VA: IHS Press, 2008), 35.
100 Senior, 35.

of course there is a risk. When brides and grooms make promises till death, they are something radically audacious that no geometer can measure, no science comprehend. Love is an act of generosity, the root of which is "generate," because intelligent life is the greatest good in nature. We want more children because the good is diffusive and love increases by giving.[101]

The risk with having more children is that, yes, the world has sin. But to heal that wound and build up humanity by love is significantly better than to subdue all that is truly human—and truly natural—into a machine that just wants to make sure there is enough cheap grain for all these mouths. As Wendell Berry humorously puts it, most environmentalists today propose the formula to solve all problems as "Technology + Political Will = the Solution."[102] But once again, we see that the place of the Catholic homestead is not only good for the family itself but a beautiful witness to the truth: that fertility is a blessing and love diffuses itself into more, not less. Our technical knowledge simply can't catch up with this truth, because it is of a different order. The pride in our worldly knowledge can too easily forget to love, to be fruitful and multiply. As Saint Paul says, "'Knowledge' puffs up, but love builds up" (1 Cor 8:1).

Saint Thomas Aquinas even says that returning to the soil will help us see again that although there is work and effort, the earth is there to provide for our needs. "For the soil gives birth to the herb of its own accord; and such like products of the earth may be had in great quantities with very little effort: whereas no small trouble is necessary either to rear or to catch an animal. Consequently, God being wishful to bring His people back to a more simple way of living, forbade them to eat many kinds of animals, but not those things that are produced by the soil."[103]

Catholic homesteads can similarly be confident that God "being wishful to bring His people back to a more simple way of living" can experience His goodness, abundance, and generosity in their direct experience of it from the land.

---

101 Senior, 25–26.
102 Wendell Berry, *The Art of Loading Brush* (Berkeley, CA: Counterpoint, 2017), 104.
103 *Summa Theologica* I-II, q. 102, art. 6, rep. 1.2.

The Land of Raw Milk and (Bartered for) Honey   *–Jason Craig*

When we first started milking cows, we were broke. However, the abundance of those two Jersey cows made us feel like kings. With such an abundance, not only were we able to eat an amazing assortment of fresh foods, but we could raise pigs very affordably from any spillage or waste from the milk, and we were also able to give away and barter with it. This experience really altered the way we understood our resources and our relationship to the needs of others.

I've been overwhelmed, in fact, at how generosity with what we produce tends to breed further generosity. When Saint Paul says to "out do one another" in love (see Rom 12:10), I think it alludes to the reality that is pregnant in the nature of things, that love and care increase as they are truly practiced. I have a neighbor who will not accept money for his abundance of eggs which he brings to us all the time. "I have enough," he says. But he'll accept butter and milk. In gratitude for that, I have given him a piglet or two, and he always helps me castrate them when it's time.

Another neighbor does all of my butchering for me, which is no small thing since we raise many hundreds of pounds of meat in pigs and cows. I don't pay him for it because he comes and gets milk whenever he needs it. Others bring vegetables to trade or just because they have so many.

We know summer is fully here when a local farmer drives around to homesteaders and friends to give away his seemingly endless supply of watermelon that he grows on the side.

We've learned that we can get much more honey from bartering butter than we can by raising bees.

It isn't quite the case that none of this should be accounted for in any way. Good accounting makes good friends, as I've heard it put. But although we should be careful to always avoid any injustice, it is still a truth that we learn by doing that there isn't just enough for all to eat, but there's more than we need. We would not know that, however, without learning how to be generous ourselves, learning to receive with gratitude the generosity of others, and seeing how our mutual care for each other's needs dispels the myth that we are alone and are doing what is best when we just care for ourselves.

DISCERNING A PLACE
BETWEEN SUBURBIA
AND THE VILLAGE

As we've seen, the historic drift from a predominately homesteading or land-based economy—where homes are places of both production and, to differing degrees, consumption—is a general move toward a more *suburban* economic makeup.

Therefore, we place before us the word "suburban" home not as a slur or degradation but as an observation of the predominant arrangements for most households in our country. And, relatedly, this is very often the thing that people are moving *away* from in a desire to move *toward a homestead*. This shows that, for many, the urging toward a homestead is not necessarily a romantic and impractical idealizing of a bygone era but an *essentially practical* reorientation of the home as an economy unit, remembering again that the original meaning of the word "economy" *is* household management. We are reconceiving not just how we think of a home but what a home is *for*. We who are, in a sense, converting our homes to this different arrangement must recognize that between suburbia and a community of homesteads is a spectrum of arrangements, and making a move on that spectrum can be subtle but fruitful or it can be an entire and total change of culture.

Perhaps some can understand this conversion to a functioning home through their experience of homeschooling. The homeschool represents something very similar to the homestead because it brings the family back into union with place and each other for a good and human work that exists more predominately in a mass production model. It brings the home back into *use*. Perhaps this is why so many homesteads begin as homeschools. In speaking of one such family, Alan Carlson reports the impact on a family discovering that doing it yourself at home provides all sorts of practical freedoms: "Once again, [an] 'experiment in domestic production' proved its superiority over a mass system of production [like large public schools]. Two hours a day of course work, it turned out, was all it took for the . . . boys to keep pace with their public school counterparts, reflecting the great waste of time in group education. They also found that the remaining hours could be filled with reading and creative activities in the garden, the kitchen, and the workshop."[104]

We want your efforts at ordering your household by the logic of homesteading—the liturgy of the land—to be integrated and successful the way this family experienced ordering around the homeschool. But as any homeschooling family will tell you, the surrounding environment, temperaments of individuals, and a large array of circumstances can make the ordering of the home feel more like juggling cats. Therefore, these considerations are meant to help families—especially parents—discern a broader picture and understand the implications of homesteading.

What is critical at this juncture is that the homestead and the household that makes it what it is are shaped by the culture of those that live and work there. Cultures within a home are formed by many things, but a significant one is simply how time and money are spent, where priorities, dispositions, and desires really land. This is where the difference between the suburban home and the homestead realizes a certain tension because the cultures needed to live fully in those settings are often at odds.

Therefore, we are presuming in the following spectrums that on the fully suburban side, there is at least some desire to connect to the ideas (why else would you be reading the book?). This will show that even if a full change isn't feasible, there are ways to make the household more integrated with nature, work, and the liturgy of the land. We are also presuming that a full swing to a completely self-sustaining homestead is often very difficult for a first-generation homesteader, and we are aware that most homesteads will have other outside income. An important note here is that this is not a historical

---

104 Alan C. Carlson, *The New Agrarian Mind: The Movement Toward Decentralist Thought in Twentieth-Century America* (New York: Routledge, 2000), 63.

anomaly, as homesteaders have regularly, throughout times and cultures, engaged in other remunerative work alongside farming.

A homestead is a place of work primarily for the basics of bodily care—food, shelter, and warmth. A suburban home is not free from these needs, of course, but simply supplies them indirectly by working away from the home for an income that is used to purchase these things. For the following spectrum, we will follow the need for warmth through the use of burned fuels. We will use something like firewood, however, to show that there are bigger and bigger implications to household culture as one engages more with the liturgy of the land and less with the modern economic arrangement of suburban and urban centers in an industrialized world.

As a consideration, we will follow the use of fuel to heat a home as a specific example of how these spectrums relate. After seeing how these spectrums play out, we will provide four images of a home that might help you picture what is realistic for you and your family.

NEED FOR OFF-FARM INCOME

SUBURBIA ← higher vs. lower → HOMESTEAD

Suburban homes require a greater dependence on money itself, of outside income. The mobility necessary to engage in suburban life typically requires a car and all of the associated expenses, often multiple ones for larger families or families with multiple working adults. The activities and groups one engages with often have expenses associated with them as well. Outside of these extracurricular activities, all of the practical needs of the home are purchased and brought into the home for consumption and use. Having multiple incomes also increases that need due to the expenses of daycare, less time for food preparation, and an overall decrease in time needed to procure a different source of heat, like wood. For warmth, one usually has the predominant fuel used in your region, from natural gas to electricity. Therefore, one might reasonably purchase firewood as another input to the home and burn it in a fireplace as a way to feel and sense the connection to the land in a way that pushing the button on a thermostat does not produce. The enjoyment aspect of it is high, but the practical *need* for it is low and may even be an additional expense of time and money. Firewood is a matter of lifestyle.

On the other end of the spectrum is the homestead that heats exclusively with wood. Firewood is renewable and very often can be found at little or no cost (trees from storms, and so on). But it still takes work. That work of supplying your home with fire-wood—finding, cutting, splitting, stacking, drying, burning—is not a matter of a few cozy fires in the winter to have a nice ambiance, but it becomes a necessary occupation of time in order to stay warm. It isn't chosen but required. If you don't have the income to purchase other fuels because your off-farm income is significantly less, then your time will be spent on firewood. You will not have money for other fuels, but the tradeoff is that you don't need that money as much because your need is supplied directly.

CULTURE FORMED BY PERSONAL INTEREST, ACTIVITIES, AND CHOICES

SUBURBIA ← higher vs. lower → HOMESTEAD

In the suburban home that is more dependent on income, the many activities of work, sociability, and personal interest are often outside of the home. Much effort is spent on deciding what activities will be done by which individuals and how those varying activities will be balanced in their requirement of time and money. There are reasons that many households enjoy the suburban or urban life, not the least of which is the availability and options of off-farm activities. Sports and other extracurricular activities associated with children, for example, are plentiful in suburbia and usually dominate the use of time and money to an extent that makes those things the primary force that builds and directs the culture of a home and how time and money are spent. If your household has as its goals, custom, and disposition engagements in such activities, then this necessarily limits the time and dedication that more significant homesteading endeavors require. Therefore, you might purchase firewood instead of splitting it because you are physically tired from practices and games and simply don't have extra days to gather and split the wood. But given that many jobs are sedentary and you don't get a lot of exercise, you might decide to join a gym, which is a much more common activity in your community and provides, therefore, time for social and physical benefit as well as discipline and fitness. The gym, we must remember, is another expense, so it reinforces the requirement for outside in-come. But although the social pressure can be great in getting roped into these various activities, they still reside primarily in the place of *choice* and personal discipline.

The homestead has fewer choices. Because you need firewood for the winter—maybe even for cooking—the time you devote to that is not optional. The tradeoff of this inde-pendence from the need for the money to heat with is that you now have limited time because the wood must be split. Therefore, you might not be able to join the gym because you don't have the time or the money for it—less money because you do less off-farm work and less time because you do more on-farm work of stacking wood. But you do have warmth *and exercise*. When firewood is necessary and hard to get (and bucking logs is heavy lifting), paying to go to a place to lift heavy things becomes ridiculous and wasteful. Also, since supplying wood for a home can (and should!) be done with others, your community is formed more around others that share that need and work with you, including both families and neighbors. Therefore, one experiences belonging like that of a gym, but in a necessitated community rather than a chosen one. The more intensely one depends on his homestead for the direct supplying of needs, the less optional it becomes.

CULTURE OF INTEGRATED WORK AND TIME TOGETHER
SUBURBIA ← lower vs. higher → HOMESTEAD

The nature of suburban activities is very often based on age, personal interest, and personal abilities. A large family, for example, might have many kids in sports, but those are likely differing sports in differing age groups; this does not take into account that many parents might engage in adult leagues as well. Often, parents find themselves deciding on what activities to allow or not allow based on the perceived benefit to the formation or social life of their children or the perceived good for the family: is it an expense that is worth the time and money? Therefore, much time is spent (rightfully so) in trying to keep a balance between the members of the household and their *personal* interests and endeavors. Busy families will tell you that it requires great *intentionality*—even a fight—to keep the family doing important things together, such as prayer and meals.

The homestead has significantly more integration of time spent together as a family because the work of the home can more easily be shared, and often *must* be shared to get it done. Each member of a household knows they need to be warm in the winter; they literally feel and know the need. Since there is not time and money to do off-farm activities anyway, they join the broader work of the home economy. On wood-splitting days, the father and older kids might be splitting while the younger ones stack, for example. The options for personal interests are more limited, but with that, the unintentional disintegration of the family's time into private interests that require great balance and effort gives way to the natural, even unintentional, integration of the family through shared work and need.

CULTURE FORMED BY WORKING THE SEASONS

SUBURBIA ← lower vs. higher → HOMESTEAD

An explicit goal of the homestead is greater integration with and experience of nature it-self. In a suburban home, this must be achieved by intentionality because much of those lives are spent in artificially maintained environments of climate and activity and the surrounding culture is based on less-natural activities. For example, there is no need to wait for summertime to go swimming because indoor pools may be available at a local recreation center. Ice hockey is played through the summer. The temperature of the home is pretty steady year-round, and there is often not a significant difference even in

diet and meals throughout the year due to a globalized and processed-based food economy. If one wants to really feel and experience the changes of the season, effort might need to be given to intentionally enjoy a farmers' market instead of a grocery store, for example. In theory, a fire in the fireplace could even be enjoyed any time of year if the primary purpose is ambiance and not actual warmth.

Clearly, the homestead is bound to the seasons and realities of the land much more. One often enjoys the act and art of gathering firewood during months when it might not actually be needed, like in early spring before the garden takes up more time but there's still good time for the wood to season before it is needed in the winter. Outside of some enterprises like aquaculture (the growing of fish and plants in a greenhouse in an enclosed and highly engineered system), one experiences and works the land not based on choice and desire but based on the needs and work that come naturally with the land. One might, for example, spend the cooler morning splitting wood while taking the opportunity to enjoy a nearby river in the heat of the day. Your cues for how you spend your time are based much more on nature and less on engineered, intentional, and manufactured experiences.

HOUSEHOLD NEEDS SUPPLIED FROM THE LAND

SUBURBIA ← lower vs. higher → HOMESTEAD

As we've been noting, the needs of a suburban home are rarely provided by work we would categorize as homesteading, the supplying of needs directly without the intermediary tool of money. This does not mean it is impossible. The potential for backyards to house chickens, gardens, and bees is great. However, limited time and a greater demand for off-farm work and interests make these enterprises potentially more of a strain—just another thing on the list to get done. Therefore, it is likely that only a few things can be engaged in intentionally as a way to supply those needs.

As one moves more toward the productive homestead, the needs are provided for more directly. The decrease in both options and choice increase the likelihood of having both the time and the need for providing for these needs. Therefore, the wealth of that home will be increasingly based on real things and not the ability to purchase those things. Continuing our focus on firewood, you will have the time and demand to supply warmth for the home directly.

INVESTMENT OF THE WHOLE HOUSEHOLD
SUBURBIA ← lower vs. higher → HOMESTEAD

As noted above, the suburban home is often a complex and coordinated enterprise that is born from a household of differing interests and activities. Homesteading, therefore, might actually be the interest of one or a few of them. If a family still lives in suburbia and is more engaged with that culture and economy, then very likely the interests available will pull members away to do those things. In some ways, the homestead in the backyard might be another one of these personal interests pursued by a few or even just one. This is actually more possible and can have great returns for the household because even one person with a large garden not only feeds the family but also provides the witness, goodness, and context of the liturgy of the land—even if limited in scale. If truly interested, the seasonal labor of firewood could be a great personal interest that contributes to that individual and the whole, without demanding that the whole household engage with them.

On the homestead, the sheer necessity and ubiquity of the whole endeavor necessitate the engagement of most or all of the family. Even if the work falls primarily to, say, the father or some older children, the necessity of these endeavors—because they are part of the home's essential provision—makes them the dominant factor in coordinating the life of the home. Therefore, the more one needs the firewood, the greater the likelihood that everyone must be fully bought in and active in the life and culture of it.

SECURE ACCESS TO LAND
SUBURBIA ← lower vs. higher → HOMESTEAD

Suburban homes often have enough land for very robust backyard homesteads. Since the constraints of time and resources require the homesteading to be on a smaller scale, access to larger portions of land is not as necessary and a greater focus on intensive use is better. Many suburban and urban locations even have land set aside for community and private plots.

On the homestead, there is obviously a greater need for access to land. However, note that we use the term *access* and not *ownership*. Depending on the enterprises that one focuses on, there is still a great possibility of growing much of your own food on a small plot of owned land while only needing greater access to other land. Also

depending on the enterprises, this access can be more or less secure, meaning long-term and unchanging. For example, many people, especially in rural locations, can find large pastures to rent for livestock. In that case, the need for security is greater because the investment of time and money means that if this access were somehow lost, the impact would be much greater. Access to forests for collecting firewood is relatively easy to find, but even simpler is to be aware of and in communication with your local community about the regular ability to find downed trees and other "waste" that you can gather and process for your family for little to no cost. This is not secured land but very helpful in their abundance for shorter time periods.

COMPETENCY IN MANUAL ARTS AND LAND-WORKING SKILLS

SUBURBIA ← lower vs. higher → HOMESTEAD

Suburban homes often look very similar, but the work and income of those inside them have a great variety. Often, one can have a neighbor whose income and technical training is a complete mystery. Also, the training and skills employed for those jobs are likely honed by education, experience, training, and a general upward movement within various industries and segments of the economy, from a hotel manager to a financial planner. Because those jobs have a high level of expertise and have been pursued often from a very young age—being trained from school years through college up through internships and so on—there may have been limited exposure and experience with the manual skills necessary for homesteading. This might mean, for example, that one might not even know how to split wood properly, and the competency barrier may be more significant. However, because the homestead endeavors in a suburban backyard are not absolutely necessary to the actual economy of the home, the learning curve is not a problem but rather part of the enjoyment and value of the effort.

Homesteads *require* a wide range of skills and competencies. If you don't know them, you would have to pay for them, which is not always an option and is even in conflict with the reality of the homestead. Farmers are famous for having a broad skillset, from electrical work to animal husbandry. They have to read the weather, know when or when not to work the soil, and know when a seed catalog is completely exaggerating the return of a new variety of corn. Without experience and competency, a homestead can be a challenge bordering on the impossible if there is no ability to learn fast through mentors, effort, and a natural propensity for manual work. Some do not have proper reverence for the time and effort it takes to gain manual competency, and they presume too much on their ability to be able to just pick it up whenever they want, despite being ignorant and incapable. In fact, there is great danger and risk if one creates a situation of dependence on a homestead but not the skill and know-how to meet that need. If one is unable to procure and process firewood, for example, then the lack of ability can turn from provision through work to another expense and danger.

FOUR SCENARIOS

These considerations of how homesteading frees you to do some things and limits you from others can save you from many potential frustrations. Without some discernment and discussion, you may find yourself always feeling like you're not doing enough homesteading or enough in other areas of life, like remunerative work and recreation. We clearly recognize that there is a conflict between suburban life and the homestead, but that doesn't mean that one is completely limited; it just means that we should be careful in recognizing those differences. Also, recognizing where you might land on the spectrum can help you in very practical ways so that homesteading becomes something provisional for your home and not just another drain on time and resources like any other interest or hobby.

We should note that the rise in at-home, remunerative work has greatly increased (remote work), which has increased the potential for homesteading even in a suburban or urban setting—or even making a move to a more rural place feasible. But you might discern that you are not willing to give up certain activities—gyms, sports, associations, and so on—and, therefore, you should be careful not to create a situation where you might live on a homestead outside of town but spend most of your time driving into town and, therefore, less time with your family and land. In that case, the land might increasingly become a burden, and your stewardship of that land might be lacking. In other words, you don't want to end up with a large but neglected garden, a longer drive to soccer practice, and a greater strain on time and money than before. This won't bring the peace and integration of the family you hoped for, but it could bring strife and division. This would work against the purpose and culture of the homestead itself.

Most people will likely find themselves moving through stages on the spectrum toward the homestead. We do not mean to propose that these changes can or should happen all at once. Both of us experienced different evolutions and seasons of homesteading, and we don't at all think that we are totally settled with our conversion toward homesteading, but that is our explicit direction.

Gathering our own experience and the observations of many friends and neighbors, we think that you can consider roughly four scenarios taken from this spectrum which we offer you as a way to see where you are or maybe chart a path toward homesteading, or even simply settling into an intentional balance.

THE BACKYARD GARDENER

- Likely lives in a suburban environment.
- Requires one or more full-time incomes that are likely connected to the local place (like an office in the city).
- Likely located within a reasonable distance of suburban amenities and shopping.
- Few homestead endeavors so as to allow more mobile and active (off-farm) activities.
- Does not require all members of the home to be engaged in homesteading.
- Cultural dominance comes from off-farm activities and work.
- Minimal financial impact from what is produced or grown.
- Low but meaningful engagement with growing and cultivation.
- Low need for land access.
- Lower need for manual competency.

THE HOBBY HOMESTEADER

- May have a larger suburban lot or live at the edge of town.
- Requires only one full-time job, perhaps done remotely.
- Could be located further from amenities, which are engaged less than typical suburbia.
- More homestead endeavors but kept limited and in balance with work and off-farm activities.
- More than one member of the household engaged on the homestead.
- Culture of the home kept in more of a balance between in-town and on-farm.
- Moderate financial impact from what is grown on the farm.
- Meaningful engagement with growing and cultivation.
- Low to moderate need for land access.
- Low to moderate need for manual competency.

THE SIDELINE SUPPLEMENTER

- Might live on the edge of town or in a more rural setting.
- Requires one or more part-time jobs, perhaps full-time remote work.
- Likely located in a more rural or distanced property.
- Significant dedication to homestead endeavors.
- Culture formed predominately from homesteading.
- Requires that most members of the household be engaged in homesteading.
- High impact of homestead-produced goods on finances.
- Predominant and meaningful engagement with growing and cultivation.
- Moderate need for land access.
- Moderate to high need for manual competency.

FULL-TIME HOMESTEADER

- Likely live more rural.
- Requires part-time or occasional outside income.
- Goods from the homestead are the dominant financial consideration.
- Culture of homesteading is completely dominant, perhaps venturing into full-time farming.
- Requires all members to be integrated and "bought-in" to homesteading culture.
- Homestead endeavors fully dominate time, significantly limiting ability for other activities.
- Dominant engagement with homesteading and a community based on farming.
- Greater need for moderate to large land access and security.
- High need for manual competency.

In each of these scenarios, we can recognize friends and neighbors. We have friends with acreage in a city where they keep a milk cow. We know homesteaders that have very little land but lease acreage in order to supply most of their food. We know families where the father is on board with supporting the work of a wife and kids that work a homestead, but he cannot engage much due to his off-farm job.

We can also see that preexisting conditions play a large role in what is feasible. Some people might have an inheritance or outside investment that makes the initial purchase and start-up of a homestead possible. Others might have family members joining them in the expense and work of starting. Others are simply limited in where they can go and, therefore, intentionally order their lives around a small but robust backyard farm. Questions about mortgages, debt, and risk are important and impactful. Not everyone will be willing or able to be full-time on their land. These scenarios are not set in stone but represent a realistic view of what forms the culture and work of your homestead.

FROM INDEPENDENCE TO INTERDEPENDENCE

"None of us is individually self-sufficient, but each has many needs he can not satisfy."

—PLATO[104]

"For man's productive effort cannot yield its fruits unless a truly social and organic body exists, unless a social and juridical order watches over the exercise of work, unless the various occupations, being interdependent, cooperate with and mutually complete one another, and, what is still more important, unless mind, material things, and work combine and form as it were a single whole."

—POPE PIUS XI[105]

New homesteaders often find themselves defending their move toward the land to others specifically in the truth and need of our social bonds. After all, is not a move to the land a move away from society as it is today? As we have been presenting in this book, there are foundational philosophies of the homestead that do conflict with the modern world, mostly in the necessity and importance of a home independent from the artificial economy and forms of dependence that do not lend themselves to healthy households.

---

105 Plato, *Republic*, 369b.
106 Pius XI, Encyclical *Quadragesimo Anno* (May 15, 1931), no. 69.

We want to live closer to creation itself so as to sense and experience what God says through it. Therefore, we limit, remove, and turn away from the artificial. We turn toward God. We turn toward our family. We turn toward the land. Sometimes those who remain in places like suburbia feel that we have turned away from them and that the independence of the homesteader is a form of separation from our brothers and our communities. We admit there can be conflicts in the social ways we have left behind because people whose cultures are formed by different forces can find it harder to integrate their lives together.

But it would be very wrong to think that the homesteader, by definition, is seeking radical independence from others. Materially speaking, the independence of the homestead has to do with natural security in the necessary goods of nature and independence from the artificial economy and its excesses, false promises, and abuses. This is what is meant by independence, for example, in titles of books like *The Independent Homestead*, which was written by Catholic authors Shawn and Beth Dougherty. Perhaps ironically, given the title, that book not only does a great job of showing how to farm in accord with nature, but it also makes clear that the homestead's reliance on nature actually creates a greater reliance on others. Homesteads don't make you independent but rather reveal and encourage interdependence: "[Our] friends, our community, are more important in the daily business of our lives than we have ever imagined them to be before [starting the farm]. The example, aid, and comradeship of other grass-based farmers . . . have demonstrated our dependence on the help, advice, and friendship of other people. Butchering four hogs in a weekend, we are glad for all the people to show up to share the labor, time-honored jokes, good food. . . . Farmers need friends; those tough frontiersmen who did it all themselves probably died young."[107]

We must also note that it is a Catholic doctrine that man is a social animal. Not only do we need community because we are wired that way, as they say, but because it is in belonging to a *body* that we are saved. That is, we are bound to one another as a body because we belong to Jesus Christ, and His Body is the Church, a true and visible society of people. Yes, salvation comes to each individual through the personal workings of grace,

---

107 Shawn and Beth Dougherty, *The Independent Farmstead: Growing Soil, Biodiversity, and Nutrient-Dense Food with Grassfed Animals and Intensive Pasture Management* (White River Junction, VT: Chelsea Green Publishing, 2016), 296.

but God has clearly ordained that part of our restoration in Christ is to be restored to one another through the virtue of charity. St. Thomas Aquinas calls charity a single virtue, but one that is expressed in two ways: the love of God and the love of neighbor, as Our Lord taught quite simply. We cannot truly love God and not love our neighbor, and we cannot love our neighbor fully if we do not love God. Our dependence on one another begins at conversion when, after assenting in faith to God's invitation, we must be baptized. As the very sacramental foundation of the spiritual life, we should note that at the very beginning of our spiritual lives, we are dependent on others because one cannot baptize himself.

The Church recognizes that in the social order, man's working of the land, his prayer, and the ordering of households are all designed by God to be brought into a harmonious whole, with each part not working for some abstract good, like efficiency, but working together as a living body. It is false to attempt to exclude our economic life and our spiritual life since man is both economic and spiritual at the same time. They integrate together in the reality of living and cannot be understood in isolation from the other. "If all these relations are properly maintained," said Pope Pius XI, "the various occupations will combine and coalesce into, as it were, a single body and like members of the body mutually aid and complete one another."[108]

INTERDEPENDENCY

The mutual dependency of the spiritual life as lived in the Church is reflected in both directions on the homestead. As one encounters the independence of the homestead, what occurs naturally—by the very nature of the natural economy—is actually *interdependence*. The homestead, if compared with more commercial operations of modern farms, relies on an even greater interdependence. Someone who raises pigs likely needs supplemental feeds, so they might get to know a local feed mill. Limitations of time and know-how might also create the need to know a local butcher. And even if you can do it yourself, the act of hog-killing is an essentially social tradition and custom that involves the whole family and your neighbors as well. Sometimes, the social and practical value of your neighbors creates the kind of bonds that are truly familial, becoming better than those we love that are physically distant from the functional household of the homestead, as Proverbs says: "Better is a neighbor who is near than a brother who is far away" (Prv 27:10).

Our cultivation and consideration of the earth's abundance, in fact, is always something that tends toward justice, which is man's right relationship with man. As Thomist Christopher Thompson puts it: "The tradition of natural law, so ably defended for centuries by Roman Catholic theologians and philosophers, supplies insights into how environmental stewardship ought to be properly conducted. The natural law tradition would affirm not only the dignity and value of the various creatures and our relationship to them, but it would begin to outline more completely how human beings are to treat the environment within the context of just relationship with one another."[109]

Stewarding land teaches us a proper relationship with the earth that counteracts the excesses of those who would abuse humans in the name of environmentalism and also those who would isolate themselves from each other due, in part, to their distance from creation.

---

108 Pius XI, Encyclical *Quadragesimo Anno* (May 15, 1931), no. 75.
109 Christopher Thompson, *The Joyful Mystery* (Steubenville, OH: Emmaus, 2017), 45.

NATURAL COMMUNITY

In fact, we can see quite clearly that the isolation from each other, so prevalent in a society that consistently reports a growing sense of loneliness, is not solved merely by living close to other people in suburban or urban centers.

The danger of a household's independence, therefore, does not occur from dependence on the land for food but from its *lack of dependence* on others. Isolation is made possible principally by the financial independence of a home that is structured from and toward the artificial economy of money. In the average suburb, for example, associations of people—their social lives with neighbors and community—are created by choice and effort. They do not *need* one another in the fuller human sense that includes economics and shared work. You can live alongside people for a lifetime

without knowing, understanding, or even really caring about what they do for a living. It has no bearing on the community. Suburban neighborhoods are arranged not by kinship or tradition but by socioeconomic status—income levels. This is not to say that their bonds are meaningless, but they come by intentionality and not by the natural course of shared work directly related to the foundational needs of food and shelter. This might indicate that despite the charge of isolationism, it is the suburban and urban models that constitute greater disaffiliation and distance from meaningful social bonds.

In Robert Nisbet's *The Quest for Community*, he brings to question whether the chosen associations of modern times can even really be compared to the shared customs, traditions, and bonds that were born naturally and necessarily from former agrarian times:

> The Common assumption that, as the older associations of kinship and neighborhood have become weakened, they are replaced by new voluntary associations filling the same role is not above sharp question. The traditional groups have weakened in significance is apparently true enough but, on the evidence, their place has not been taken to an appreciable extent by new forms of associations. Despite the appeal of older sociological stereotypes of the urban dweller who belongs to various voluntary associations, all of which have progressively replaced the older social unities, the facts so far gathered suggest the contrary; that a rising number of individuals belong to no organized association at all, and that, in the large cities, the unaffiliated persons may even constitute a majority of the population.[110]

Therefore, the homesteader must learn to see and depend on God more, recognizing His hand in the order of creation. The homesteader also more fully realizes his need for his whole household, for as the fruitfulness of the land increases, so does the need for shared responsibility and integration. And the homesteader comes to treasure his people and place—what is around him—from a shared affection and bond that is both affectionate and practical. There is, of course, human agency and intentionality in this,

---

110 Robert Nisbet, *The Quest for Community* (Wilmington, DE: ISI Books, 2014), 63.

but it is not decided on by a recognition that it would be a good thing to do as much as from the natural and consequential need for one another. If there is a sense of isolation on the homestead, this is a defect.

BUDDING COMMUNITIES

All that being said, new homesteaders will likely find that working closer to the land does not immediately produce a healthy community. Homesteaders rightly understand themselves as pioneering a new way of life at odds with modern society. This brings with it some separation from old social ties, especially if one moves away physically. And a true pioneer—one who sets out ahead of others—will naturally find himself alone. The leaders and families that set out during the English Catholic Land Movement understood this pioneering spirit and its challenges. "It has fallen to the Catholic Land Movement," said Fr. H. E. G. Rope, "to be the *pioneers* of the Exodus from that urban slough of despond which appalls every right-minded person."[111] They understood civilization to have been essentially lost to industrialism, and they were therefore starting over. That quote was published in the 1930s, and that movement was largely undone by World War II and the massive increase of industrialization after the war as various industries repurposed their factories from weapons to other products. We are right to understand the homesteading movement of today to be in a related situation, of starting again within the shell of something that couldn't care less or even disdains the whole project of it. Our American tradition and history mean that we have similar principles, but our situation and work will be different. One similarity, however, will be the truth that we are attempting to rebuild the great achievement of Christendom, which is the Catholic village.

Therefore, homesteading begins in the practical production of goods for a household, but the Catholic must understand it for what it truly is, a project of a *cultural* sort. There are some who will set out and may find themselves feeling like a voice in the proverbial wilderness, calling people out of something, yes, but also to something. If possible, this invitation should be made explicit, with love and prudence, so that others can find practical paths to the culture of homesteading, meaning a way of life shared with others.

---

111 H. E. G. Rope, *Flee to the Fields* (Norfolk, VA: HIS Press 2003), 132, emphasis added.

Catholics are a people that always start with the basics but never stop there. Food is not just brought up from the ground and grazed off in imitation of the beasts but prepared into a meal and served on a table to be shared with others. That table is surrounded by people who love one another and do so specifically in enjoying the goods of the earth together. A meal shared is always an act of culture because, although it starts with the natural need for food, it is surrounded by ceremony, other people, and prayer. We cannot imagine Catholic culture without the meal, for the signs and ceremonies of God's covenants with man—from the lamb at Passover to the Paschal Lamb of God at Easter—have in mind meals as signs and seals of salvation. As the work and interdependence of homesteads grow up from the basics provided by working with nature, it is met with the grace of God and the truth of the Church. This intersection of flesh and spirit is the place where true culture springs up.

Similarly, our homesteads begin with our households, but we long for and need others to bring about the full maturity of our little farms. To sow and reap is not a complete act. They are brought to completion with an expression of gratitude to God, a loving preparation and presentation, and enjoying them with others. This is what makes it the true liturgy of the land.

We sincerely hope that the preceding chapters did not seem in any way esoteric. We know that we did not get into the nitty-gritty of when to plant corn or how to skin a hog (don't skin them; rather, scald and scrape them!). The reality is that the homestead represents a fundamental shift not just in the work of the hands but in the work of the mind and soul. We have been tuned by a society that is explicitly opposed to the Church, devoid of the natural world. The implicit modes of thought in secularism, modernism, industrialism, and other -isms seep in and form us. Without a conversion to the liturgy of the land, we may very well bring those disorders to the land and our families as we attempt to bring those two together.

That being said, we do want to offer some practical considerations. We have in mind here not primarily the retiree who can afford to homestead, purchase the land, tools, infrastructure, and so on, and hop into it without significant threat to their long-term financial security. We are not dismissive of such people and are grateful to call them neighbors. However, the young or more financially insecure family taking a risk with a new life represents something different because if they fail, the longer-term implications can be more far-reaching. For them, mistakes are more costly, disorder is more disruptive, and disunion of wills is more damaging to the relationships we want to strengthen by homesteading.

DISCERNING IDEAS
AND ENTERPRISES

"The endeavor [or work] sums up the most important tempo-
ral elements of the universal good—the satisfaction of physical
needs to that man may, without hindrance, devote himself to
the worship of God. In this highest of goods, which is eternal
salvation, the needs of all men find their fulfillment." [112]

—STEFAN CARDINAL WYSZYNKI

INTEGRATED INTO PLACE, AN EXAMINATION

How we view our time as a family on the homestead, the design of the home, and the surrounding gardens and pastures ought to point to something greater than ourselves and modern economics. True happiness on earth is directly correlated with pursuing what is good, true, and beautiful. Cultivating these qualities over time into our homestead will continually be a wellspring of new life and a reminder of our eternal end. This does not mean our homestead must be an idyllic garden of endless flowers from day one, be devoid of any modern efficiency to simplify the work, or have unsightly and unfinished projects waiting for more time or funds. Rather, the goal is developing a vision for the land, based on what the land needs intermingled with what our family needs, and

---

112 Stefan Cardinal Wyszynki, *All You who Labor: Work and the Sanctification of Daily Life* (Manchester, NH: Sophia Institute Press), 36.

cultivating it in that manner with a goal over time, even decades, that the homestead will reflect a beauty and goodness that inspires contemplation of God and His creation.

The life and work of the Catholic homestead ought to cultivate virtue in those that live there, and this is how we measure the true health of our home economy on a homestead. Virtue is simply the good life, a life lived in accord with truth, goodness, and beauty. Our homesteads, therefore, should be good for our faith, for our family, and for our land. To test and discern our efforts, we should always keep in mind the health of these three things. We offer these as a sort of discernment and examination.

FAITH

We must hold before our homes the truth that our first and primary purpose is to reach and glorify God in this life, which includes the life of our homestead. God is man's last end and his true and lasting happiness. If our effort at homesteading is not making us more humble, prayerful, and devout, then we are missing something critical to what it means to be a homesteading Catholic. The very purpose of our work is not worldly advancement or success but the glory of God. Today, man satisfies one want or need only to move on to the next, without end or intention. Our toil on the homestead satisfies the needs of created nature *so that* we may more attentively attend to our super-nature, as Stefan Cardinal Wyszynki wrote: "The endeavor [or work] sums up the most important temporal elements of the universal good—the satisfaction of physical needs so that man may, without hindrance, devote himself to the worship of God. In this highest of goods, which is eternal salvation, the needs of all men find their fulfillment."[113]

PROVISION

Our first practical goal of the homestead is to feed and care for our family by participating directly in growing their food. Therefore, an important question is if your interests and endeavors on the homestead are actually supplying a need for the family from the land. This may seem obvious, but there are tendencies to accept and start all sorts of animals and plants only to find yourself essentially taking care of pets and keeping a lawn mowed. Throughout most of history, all homes produced at least some of their own food, and homesteaders regularly performed other jobs and trades to help round out

---

113 Stefan Cardinal Wyszynki, *All You who Labor: Work and the Sanctification of Daily Life* (Manchester, NH: Sophia Institute Press), 36.

their livelihoods. It is we modern men—who have grown so distant from nature and so specialized in our work—that are unique in not having a greater variety of occupations, especially working the land. Cardinal Wyszynki, again, connects work, even homesteading specifically, with holiness when he points out how likely it was Our Lord Himself was a homesteader as we are using the word: "For it was the custom in the Holy Land for every small artisan to supplement his income by cultivating a small plot of ground from which he derived the most basic means of life."[114] Carpentry was His trade, but homesteading was the unspoken way of life for most. This is, in fact, why we are using that word in the place of "farming" in most instances, because the homestead is oriented specifically to the needs of a single family as its first purpose.

LAND

Third, our homesteads must be good for our land. To be destructive toward creation by hubris, neglect, or even ignorance is something we must avoid. Violence is an act that hinders or destroys the nature of something, and the work Adam was commanded to

---

114 Wyszynki, 18.

do—which we continue—was a continuation of the creative and life-giving work of God. Our work is to till and keep, not till and lose. Our work should therefore not be destructive. E. F. Schumacher (who converted to Catholicism after years of advocating for a more virtuous economy) connected our willingness to harm and abuse land with a spiritual sickness—economics as if God did not exist. He said the harm to the soil comes when "we have no firm basis of belief in meta-economic values," which he said makes abuse of land "inevitable": "How could it be otherwise? Nature, it has been said, abhors a vacuum, and when the available 'spiritual space' is not filled by some higher motivation, then it will necessarily be filled by something lower—by the small, mean, calculating attitude to life which is rationalized in the economic calculus."[115]

We would add that this disposition of care for land extends to the community approximate to us. The Church teaches that the ownership and use of land are not absolute, specifically in the sense that while we can retain and preserve the rights to a property, its connection to the common good and care of our neighbor must remain a factor in its use.

These three measures—faith, family, and land—might seem quaint and obvious. In our own experience and observation, however, being attentive to the health of these things is critical. We have seen fathers drag their reluctant families to the countryside only to live in constant tension and resentment due to a lack of integrated work and relationships. The devotional and even sacramental life of a family can suffer if the workload and location of a homestead are too much or too far from parish life or other Catholics. We have seen the strain when a family tries to live in the country but continues a suburban life (just a longer drive to soccer) to the detriment, neglect, or abuse of their land, where livestock and gardens don't constitute a way of life but simply become another task to do. We have seen fathers keep in-town jobs only to spend their entire weekend in frantic maintenance of a too-large tract that turns into a pit of time and money to the neglect of family, land, and neighbor. Bringing these concerns to the forefront is a necessary part of growing toward and on your homestead.

With each chapter of this book, we have tried to do that labor which is often harder than the physical labor of work, which is to think well. There are plenty of books about

---

115 Quoted in Joseph Pearce, *Small is Still Beautiful: Economics as if Families Mattered* (Wilmington, DE: ISI Books, 2006), 192.

the skill and art of homesteading, but we wanted to situate it within the Catholic mind and heart, coming from and leading to life in God.

However, there are specific enterprises that one might engage in to begin or add to their homesteading adventures. We present them here in a way that is likely different from many books—which focus on how to do them—and consider why we would consider this or that animal, plant, and so on. Our consideration is not in the potential profitability, nor is it solely in the efficiency of it, but in the consideration of the family as a functional and productive household. Specifically, we give perspective and rank how each potential focus can best suit a novice homesteading family.

HOW TO READ THE RATINGS

In rating each area of focus, we used ten different criteria. Most of the emphasis (75 percent of the total equation) is on what we see as the five most important criteria for a new homesteading family. Those are the family friendliness of the enterprise (20 percent of the total equation), the economic value it brings to the family (20 percent), the general learning curve (15 percent), the usual start-up expenses (10 percent), and the weekly time requirements (10 percent). The remaining 25 percent of the equation is split between the acreage requirements (5 percent), seasonal variance (5 percent), ongoing production expense (5 percent), bartering value (5 percent), and harvest requirements (5 percent). We don't look at these enterprises with an end goal of profitability or something that could be scaled up to a true business. This isn't to say that you couldn't scale up to that, but we are focused here on (a) what each enterprise requires of the land and home and (b) the functional value for the home, the return if you will, especially regarding bringing food to the family.

Another thing to keep in mind is perspective. These enterprises are scored more favorably for the smaller homestead, which we define as less than twenty acres. If you have two hundred acres of pasture that you need to manage, your preferences will look a bit different from a family with three acres of woodlands. Your personal interests will obviously carry a significant weight in which enterprises you pursue, but since it's nearly impossible to weigh that, we have left it out. To understand our perspective and weight on each of the parameters, we have sketched our faithful fictitious family to have the following characteristics:

- New to homesteading (0–3 years).
- Has a family with (younger) children.
- Lives on ten acres or less with a mix of pasture and woodlands.
- Is cost-conscious and looking to maximize value but also enjoyment as a family.
- Has a day job/self-employment and children in school or homeschooled, both of which limit available time.

The higher the number we assign to the endeavor and its associated criteria, the more it fits our fictitious family profile.

It's also worth noting that the goal is not to do everything on your homestead. It will not only stretch your time and resources thin and can cause burn-out and quickly turn the homesteading experience into a homesteading nightmare, especially in the early years. When we were starting out, it was suggested to us to initially focus on two to three enterprises at most and then consider adding a new enterprise once a year if the time, interest, and money allows. When selecting two to three to begin with, consider personal interest, ease of entry, and available resources (time, land, mindshare, etc.).

HOW WE SCORED THE ENTERPRISES

Here's how we define these areas and why we have included them.

Daily/Weekly Time Requirement (10%)

This refers to the time required to keep the enterprise productive and healthy, or simply how much daily and weekly maintenance it requires. This parameter is not counting start-up time or harvest time but only routine maintenance and tending.

A ranking of 1 indicates a high daily time requirement. A ranking of 10 indicates a low time requirement.

Start-Up Expense (10%)

All homesteading enterprises can be done with salvaged materials on the cheap or a turnkey system can be purchased from the local feed store at a higher price. We will tend toward the presumption of the DIY route but still take into consideration both time and capital to establish the particular venture. Major capital expenses such as acreage, power, water access (wells), or road access are not included in the individual enterprise weight because those considerations vary greatly based on how you have arrived on the land (lease, inheritance, mortgage, etc.).

A ranking of 1 indicates a high start-up expense. A ranking of 10 indicates a low start-up expense.

RANGE	
SCORE	EXPENSE
0-1	$5000+
2-3	$3000 - $5000
4-5	$1000 - $3000
6-7	$ 500 - $1000
8-9	$ 300 - $ 500
10	$ 0 - $ 300

Family Friendliness (20%)

We look at how easily a family with young children can approach the venture. For example, with livestock, we considered the size of the animal, its nature, how much handling it needs, and how many practical chores can be accomplished by children between the ages of five and twelve without close adult supervision. In addition, we considered if it requires or benefits from multiple people being involved.

A ranking of 1 indicates it is not friendly for families with small children. A ranking of 10 indicates it is friendly to families with small children.

Cash Value to Family (20%)

This metric considers how much a venture might save money through its value and labor requirements. What does it cost to buy the end product at the store with a post-income tax salary and sales tax? We look at the true value of this parallel economy when goods are produced on the homestead. For example, potatoes are very laborious to harvest and are very cheap from a store. Lettuce and greens, on the other hand, are very easy to harvest but can be expensive from the store. Based on that, a household might decide to purchase potatoes in bulk but grow their greens. We also consider how many additional products can be produced from a single enterprise. For example, a cow can give beef, but a milk cow can give milk, butter, yogurt, and ice cream.

A ranking of 1 indicates high cost savings. A ranking of 10 indicates low cost savings.

Learning Curve (15%)

This metric considers the required knowledge and experience base needed to successfully manage the venture. We look at how long it typically takes to acquire the experience and also the risk of failure if one lacks that experience. More exotic or eccentric livestock, for example, might have more delicate natures than a stout and sturdy animal, like a pig.

A ranking of 1 indicates a high learning curve. A ranking of 10 indicates a small learning curve.

Acreage Requirements (5%)

This metric looks at how much space is required to operate the venture to a scale that has meaningful returns for the family.

A ranking of 1 indicates a large acreage requirement. A ranking of 10 indicates a small acreage requirement.

Season Variance (5%)

This metric looks at variance in work and attention and how that might change (increase or decrease) based on the seasons. More value is placed on the seasonal variance due to the possibility of stacking enterprises that don't need constant work or attention and the ability to take breaks from them.

A ranking of 1 indicates little to no seasonality. A ranking of 1 indicates the work load is highly seasonal.

Production Expense (5%)

This metric considers the cost of the inputs and expenses like feed, treatments, seed, or other demands for money to produce the good. Does the venture require other off-farm inputs, like fuel? The higher this is scored here indicates a lower production expense—that is, better for the cost-conscious family.

A ranking of 1 indicates a high production expense. A ranking of 10 indicates a low production expense.

Harvest Requirement (5%)

This metric considers if harvesting requires specialized equipment, storage, or workspace. It also considers how much time and labor is required to harvest and the expense if the harvest is outsourced to a local specialist. It is likely, for example, that a new homesteader would need a butcher's help to harvest a full-sized beef cow. The higher the score, the simpler to harvest.

A ranking of 1 indicates very specialized harvest equipment/skill. A ranking of 10 indicates simple, low-tech harvesting equipment and skill required.

Bartering Value (5%)

This last metric considers the demand for the product in both good economic times and poor economic times. Is it abundant or scarce? Can it be value-added with relative ease to command higher bartering power (e.g., raw beeswax into candles, cream to butter, etc.). The higher the score the better the bartering value.

A ranking of 1 indicates low bartering value, typically perceived as a commodity. A ranking of 10 indicates the product is rare and highly demanded in the bartering/cash market.

ENTERPRISE COMPARISON

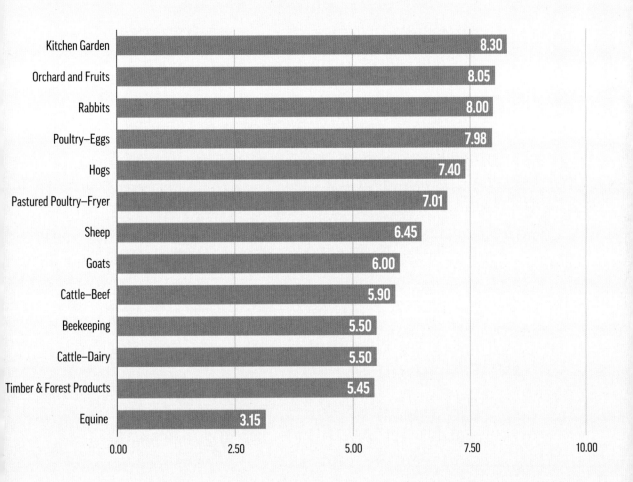

Enterprise	Value
Kitchen Garden	8.30
Orchard and Fruits	8.05
Rabbits	8.00
Poultry–Eggs	7.98
Hogs	7.40
Pastured Poultry–Fryer	7.01
Sheep	6.45
Goats	6.00
Cattle–Beef	5.90
Beekeeping	5.50
Cattle–Dairy	5.50
Timber & Forest Products	5.45
Equine	3.15

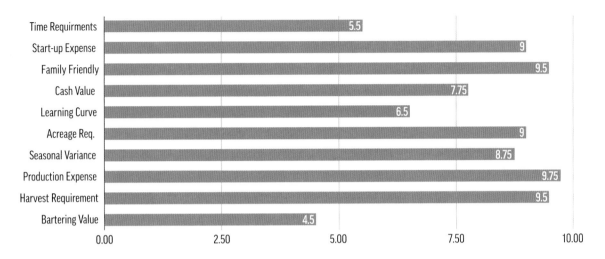

KITCHEN GARDEN

Time Requirments	5.5
Start-up Expense	9
Family Friendly	9.5
Cash Value	7.75
Learning Curve	6.5
Acreage Req.	9
Seasonal Variance	8.75
Production Expense	9.75
Harvest Requirement	9.5
Bartering Value	4.5

Kitchen Garden (8.3)

Daily/Weekly Time Requirement (5.5)

Gardens can be planted and left alone, but if you want an abundant harvest, they will need regular attention. Bed preparations, planting, cultivating, mulching, watering, and harvesting can collectively take a considerable amount of time. More often than not, the novice gardener starts too big due to the ease of modern bed preparation (tillage) but gets overrun with weeds and managing the daily and weekly demands and determines gardening isn't worth the effort. To mitigate the challenges, we find the goal should be to start small and then build to about two hundred square feet per person in the family on the upper end if you are looking to provide the majority of your seasonal veggies for the family. When we first started gardening, I used to think I had to get the garden planted all at once for the season; however, it is actually a benefit to stagger the preparations and planting out over time. Not only does this simplify the planting but also provides a succession of fresh veggies during the entire season. Planning to work in the garden for thirty to forty-five minutes four to five days a week can help you maintain an abundant kitchen garden and, in addition, get plenty of exercise to forgo the gym membership in town.

Start-Up Expense (9)

There are always plenty of things to buy with any endeavor, and gardening is not an exception. However, what is truly needed is rather simple: healthy soil, water, sunlight, seeds, and simple cultivation tools. Achieving healthy soil is both an art and a science that takes years to master, but we find leaning heavily on compost, manure, and cover cropping promotes biological life and healthier plant life and generally covers a multitude of sins. For water, we run half-inch PVC on top of the soil with overhead wobbler sprinklers. We find four sprinkler heads can irrigate a 30' x 40' area. Drip lines are a great option and more water-efficient; however, we found our hard water (high in iron) constantly clogged our drip lines within a season, and the cost to replace them or hook up an expensive filtration system was not worth it. For seeds, consulting a local gardener association or county extension office will typically provide a cheat sheet of seeds that do well in your area and when to plant. As for tools, a spade (shovel), rake, wheelbarrow, and colinear cultivator would be deemed essential. Other tools that are nice to have are a rear tine rototiller and a push seeder (Jang), but they are certainly not necessary. A modest green house is also a benefit for season extension, especially in more northern climates. We found plenty of neighbors with a tractor willing to do our initial till, or if you utilize the lasagna gardening (heavy mulching) method, no tilling may be necessary.

Family Friendliness (9.5)

We've all heard that kids don't eat vegetables, but they are a lot more likely to eat them if they were a part of growing them. Also, outside of brushing up against the irritating leaves of okra, most vegetables don't bite or scratch. In fact, so tender and simple is a vegetable patch that the kids are more likely to damage the plants by being too rough or walking through the rows and beds. With some patience, the kitchen garden can be an oasis for the family, and most activities can incorporate the children and provide plenty of opportunities for learning.

Cash Value to Family (7.75)

Vegetables are available in every grocery store, but home-grown and seasonal vegetables aren't really comparable. Tomatoes, for example, represent summertime since that's when they are ripe. There is no comparing the taste of a tomato grown in rich soil on your homestead. You can get them in a grocery store anytime, but they are grown in ways that greatly diminish the health and taste, and the distance it is shipped decreases freshness. Therefore, although vegetables can be cheap, the value of home-grown is significantly higher. The more tender vegetables, like greens, tend to be more expensive than tougher crops like corn and potatoes. To maximize savings, we have found our diet has to shift seasonally with what is abundant; also, planting veggies that can be frozen or fermented for offseason use can provide near year-round nourishment with exceptional taste at a fraction of the price of the store.

Learning Curve (6.5)

On the surface, gardening can be perceived as simple. However, maintaining and improving the garden may take a fair amount of trial and error, along with consulting local gardeners and reading seasonal veterans. We find that leaning on the experience and knowledge of market gardeners, like Elliot Coleman and Jean-Martin Fortier, or permaculturists, like Bill Mollison, can provide efficiency and technical insights that can benefit even the smaller-scale gardener. Vegetables can be grown in all sorts of ways, and how you grow them can increase or decrease the technical skills needed. The most important aspect is learning when and where to sow your garden. Also, gardening is one of the forms of wisdom that develops as a sort of intuition—that is, green thumbs. But if one can stick to it and observe the successes (and repeat them) and failures (and not repeat them), vegetables can make for a fairly easy venture with a high return.

Acreage Requirements (9)

For a family of six, a 1,200-square-foot garden (30' x 40') should provide for the majority of the seasonal needs. Add walk space, a composting area, and even a small greenhouse; everything can still be confined to less than 1/20 acre (roughly two thousand square feet). Outside of wandering vines, like pumpkins and melons, most vegetable plants take up very little room, usually around a square foot. Vegetables also don't have to be restricted to square plots but can be added to existing landscape beds, pots on the patio, and even trellised up a house or post. Both of us had grandparents and parents that kept backyard gardens that kept our tables overflowing with fresh vegetables. Staple crops, like corn, might need a bigger plot to have a substantial harvest, but a small but diverse bed can keep one eating during the whole growing season.

Seasonal Variance (8.75)

Part of the beauty of gardening is the seasonality. Frost-tolerant greens and roots in the early spring, tender veggies and fruits in the summer, and gourds or hardy greens in the fall make for a constantly evolving garden space and association of space, time, and labor changes. Unless one is using a greenhouse, there are long stretches where the only thing happening is the unseen work of microbes and worms in the soil. Not only does this give you breaks, but the seasonal variance is also a delight, as the majority of planting often occurs close to the joyful hope of spring and Eastertide, and the majority of harvest happens later in the growing season as you might be feeling more and more done with all that work, but you have a lot to show for it.

Production Expense (9.75)

Once the garden is established with irrigation, the ongoing production expense of vegetables depends almost entirely on one's ability and willingness to properly feed the soil. Remember, each vegetable taken away from the garden represents nutrients taken away from the soil. The soil gave you those nutrients, and you have to return them somehow. If you focus on feeding vegetables, then you will likely tend toward the expense of purchased fertilizers. If you focus on feeding the soil, then you will tend toward the production and use of compost and cover cropping. Although it is possible to purchase finished compost or the components to make it, with just a little bit of searching, the ingredients for compost can be found for free in both urban and rural environments. Kitchen scraps, grass clippings, manure from livestock, and woodchips from tree companies can all be procured at little cost. Also, any failure in the garden can be resurrected by tossing the dead or diseased plants into the compost. Seed saving is a craft that would eliminate the purchase of new seeds each year; however, we find the current limitations we have on space and time and the ease of purchasing seeds from reliable producers is worth the exchange.

Harvest Requirement (9.5)

Harvesting a kitchen garden for daily needs requires very little other than a sharp knife or a pair of pruners. When handling larger vegetables, like gourds or melons, a wheelbarrow is more than sufficient, and digging root veggies will need a spade or pitchfork. If scale increases (e.g., become a market gardener), the use of labor-saving devices (or more labor) becomes a necessity; however, for the homesteading family, harvesting the garden is generally remarkably simple.

Bartering Value (4.5)

Vegetables vary greatly in value. Some of the more exotic or laborious plants might command a greater value, like asparagus, but in general, vegetables have a lower value than sugars (honey, syrup) and protein (meat, dairy, eggs). This is likely due to the fact that when they are in season, they are abundant, and when they aren't, people are accustomed to the cheap prices at the store. You'll likely give away more squash than you'll ever barter or sell.

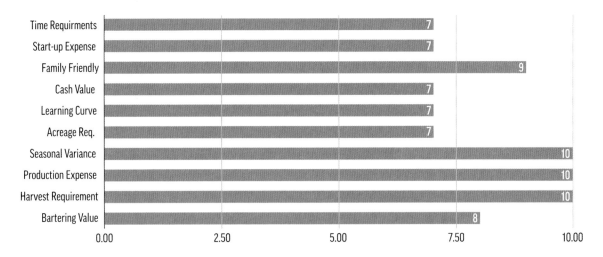

ORCHARD & FRUIT

Category	Value
Time Requirments	7
Start-up Expense	7
Family Friendly	9
Cash Value	7
Learning Curve	7
Acreage Req.	7
Seasonal Variance	10
Production Expense	10
Harvest Requirement	10
Bartering Value	8

Orchard and Fruits (8.05)

Daily/Weekly Time Requirement (7)

Once established, an orchard or berry patch has very little ongoing daily or weekly work. It's worth mulching most species as the shallow roots of grass often compete with the shallow roots of most fruit trees. The intensive work, like pruning and harvest, usually comes in short bursts and is easily managed on a Saturday afternoon when the orchard is on a small scale (1/4 acre).

Start-Up Expense (7)

The cost varies based on the size of the trees you buy. A bunch of single-stem trees purchased bare-root in bulk can be very inexpensive. A ninety-gallon potted tree can run in the hundreds of dollars. The bigger you start with, of course, means a larger harvest sooner. Unless you are at a scale or style that might require irrigation, the only expenses will be in the tree itself and any soil amendments needed, which is not optional but can be had close to free if one makes compost on the homestead. Also, although propagation usually requires some knowledge of asexual propagation (cuttings, etc.), this is a slow but affordable and enjoyable method to grow your orchard.

Family Friendliness (9)

Fruiting trees are a delight. The happy man in Scripture not only eats his figs but sits in the shade of them (see 1 Kgs 4:25). Trees bring enjoyment to the family without any risk or great difficulty.

Cash Value to Family (7)

Given the relative ease of growing and the high expense in the store, fruit has a great cash value. Although growing fruit on the homestead can require some adjustment, since the fruits are often smaller and have visual defects (due to commercial crops in stores being sprayed with chemicals and even waxed for presentation), the results are delicious. Delicate fruits, like berries and figs, can also be enjoyed in greater abundance since these are often very expensive in the store. Preserving any abundance (jam, jelly, preserves, etc.) only further increases value and cost savings into the year.

Learning Curve (7)

The initial planting has the greatest impact on the fruitfulness of a plant. Selecting species and varieties can be done by asking around your local area (not believing the over-promising catalogs), along with knowing when and how to prune. A book and a mentor will get you there quite easily.

Acreage Requirements (7)

Depending on the species, fruit requires some space but can easily be integrated with other things so as to not completely lock up an area. Trees can shade other animals, grapes can grow up porches or arbors, and fruiting shrubs like blueberries can be a part of the general landscape.

Seasonal Variance (10)

Once established, and depending on the amount of intervention you apply (like pruning and mulching), fruiting plants require very little seasonal work outside of harvesting.

Production Expense (10)

The ongoing expense for fruit is minimal. If you use compost and mulch well, there is basically no expense unless you use water and fertilizers. Some areas where songbirds or squirrels are abundant may require netting to preserve tender ripening fruits.

Harvest Requirement (10)

Harvesting fruit from the orchard on a homestead is similar to the harvest in a garden. Hands, buckets, and possibly small pruning shears or a knife are all that are needed. Depending on the height of your trees, a sturdy ladder may be required.

Bartering Value (8)

It seems small orchards are not as common as they should be in many parts of the country. Historically, the South did not provide enough chill time for traditional varieties of pome or stone fruit, but with the advent of low-chill cultivars, even the Southern homestead can enjoy fresh fruit. In these areas, especially, seasonal fruit is in high demand, and the bartering value should be strong.

RABBIT - FRYER

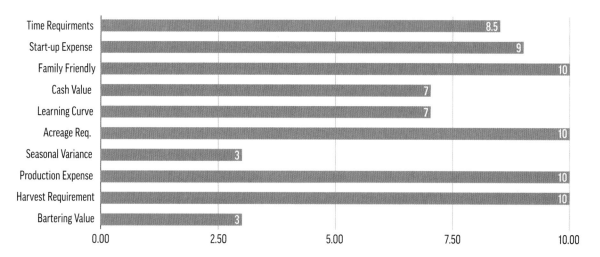

Time Requirments	8.5
Start-up Expense	9
Family Friendly	10
Cash Value	7
Learning Curve	7
Acreage Req.	10
Seasonal Variance	3
Production Expense	10
Harvest Requirement	10
Bartering Value	3

Rabbits (8)

Daily/Weekly Time Requirement (8.5)

Similar to chickens, daily chores are minimal and can be completed within ten to fifteen minutes. Our normal routine is topping off the feeders (four ounces of feed per mature doe/buck), making sure our watering system is full, and providing fresh-cut grass or high-quality hay for additional feed for the rabbits in pens. In warm weather and when the fryers (rabbits we plan to slaughter) have been weaned and are approximately six weeks old, they are moved to the pasture in a movable "Bunny Bunk," where they have an endless supply of grass and receive a new paddock each day. Moving the tractor takes less than five minutes. Once a month, depending on scale, or as necessary, the children will rake the rabbit manure from under our elevated pens where our breeding pairs live and either place the manure in the compost heap or directly in the garden. Rabbit manure has no weed seeds and is not too hot with nitrogen, so it does not burn plants. Rabbit manure provides some of the best soil on our homestead.

Start-Up Expense (9)

For less than three hundred dollars you can build five to ten pens for rabbits using J-clips and 1' x 2' hardware cloth and purchase a simple watering system and feeders for each pen from a rabbit supply house. They can easily be constructed with your children on a Saturday. Rabbits run twenty to twenty-five dollars a piece, and you will want to make sure of their sex if you plan to breed them as a meat source. We recommend referring to the Joel Salatin family (books or videos) on a visual course for constructing pens and handling rabbits.

Family Friendliness (10)

Rabbits, regardless of age, are loved by most; they are not aggressive, and they are relatively easy to handle once one understands how to securely hold them. They do have sharp nails, so if a child is not securely holding the animal, it can leave a minor (but unpleasant) scratch mark on an arm.

Cash Value to Family (7)

Rabbit meat is not often found (or pursued) in the stores for sale in America and is honestly only seen on menus of the finer white tablecloth restaurants, so it's hard to get true cash-based savings on an apples-to-apples comparison. However, we tend to compare a rabbit fryer to that of a chicken fryer. They are similar in size (two to three pounds dressed) to a dressed chicken and can easily be substituted in lieu of chicken in most recipes. The pastured rabbit has excellent taste and is low in fat (3g) and high in protein (28g) per serving. We honestly don't know why rabbit is not more a part of the American diet other than the effects of mainstream marketing on personifying the Easter Bunny. In addition to the meat from the fryer, the manure is an excellent, weed-free, high-nitrogen supplement for highly demanding annuals in your kitchen garden.

Learning Curve (7)

Rabbit care is relatively simple when compared to other animals: food, water, and shelter. If these three areas are provided and maintained, the majority of issues will be minimized. It is worth noting that rabbits are prone to heart attacks (because most of their fat encompasses their heart), so too much direct sun can cause them to overheat and result in cardiac arrest. The most complicated aspect of raising rabbits for meat is keeping track of the dates: when the doe should be bred, when they will kindle after breeding (roughly thirty days), when to wean (five to six weeks), and when to slaughter (twelve weeks). A simple notebook or calendar can solve this issue if you have one or ten breeding does. It's also worth noting that breeding rabbits has some nuance to it, and some homesteaders can have difficulty in breeding. Age, weight, air temperature, molting, and general health all impact fertility, and it's worth reading up on the details of breeding from experts before trying to grow your herd.

Acreage Requirements (10)

For the amount of protein they produce, rabbits require the least amount of space. Each breeding pair can be kept in a 2.5′ x 3′ pen that is divided into two compartments. We run one buck to seven does, and it's generally suggested to maintain, at most, a 1:10 ratio on the higher end, and for smaller producers (homesteaders), something closer to 1:5 is common. It's reasonable to breed a doe three to four times a year, with six to eight babies per kindle, netting twenty-five to thirty rabbits per doe per year. Once the rabbits are weaned and moved to pasture (warm weather) or a central pin (winter) to be grown out, the land use requirements are still minimal and can easily be incorporated into both a rural or urban homestead.

Seasonal Variance (3)

Rabbits breed best when the ambient air temperature is around 60–70°F, so depending on your local climate, some passively heated (solar greenhouse) or heated space may be needed in the winter months. When rabbits are confined in a closed space (but suspended off the floor), the ammonia from their urine can cause issues; however, providing deep manure bedding and regular disturbance (via chickens) will eliminate any smell and make wonderful compost for the following year. On our homestead in the Southeast (zone 7b–8a), the rabbits are kept under an open-air pole barn year-round. Windbreaks are provided for only the coldest of nights.

Production Expense (10)

Regular ongoing expenses are minimal when compared to other animals. Mature does and bucks require four ounces of feed per day (less than twenty-five cents) and water. In addition, nearly 70 percent of their diet can be supplemented with fresh-cut grass and mold-free hay from your homestead, further reducing input costs. It's important to give them the proper amount of food daily and not too much as overweight rabbits do not breed well.

Harvest Requirement (10)

There are a couple of different methods of slaughtering rabbits; we settled on the Bop and Bleed method as it seemed most humane and efficient, and it provides the best-tasting product from our findings. The harvest setup is simple and inexpensive: a small club (or similar), a small sharp skinning knife, and some string to hang the fryer from its feet for the bleed, skinning, and evisceration. Honestly, the hardest part is bopping (stunning) this cute cuddly critter in the proper place (behind the ears on the head), but once bopping placement is done properly, the rest of the slaughter is relatively straightforward. No machines are needed, unlike chickens, or elaborate refrigeration or a butcher shop. Rabbit, similar to beef, tastes best when allowed to age for twenty-four to forty-eight hours before serving or freezing. We typically do this in an ice water bath in coolers, but if you have access to a walk-in cooler, this could also provide the desired effect.

Bartering Value (3)

When bartering or selling pasture-raised rabbit with your neighbors, it will require (typically) a certain amount of education on the benefits of the meat, so we scored this accordingly. Americans generally do not eat rabbit, but once people realize the benefits and uses (similar to chicken), it can become an easy sell or trade.

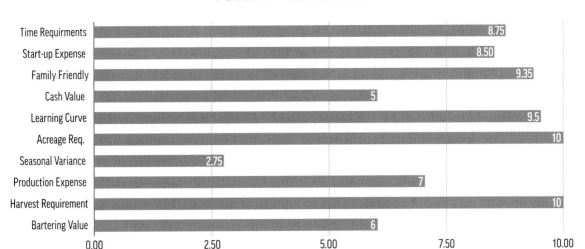

POULTRY - EGG LAYERS

Time Requirments	8.75
Start-up Expense	8.50
Family Friendly	9.35
Cash Value	5
Learning Curve	9.5
Acreage Req.	10
Seasonal Variance	2.75
Production Expense	7
Harvest Requirement	10
Bartering Value	6

0.00   2.50   5.00   7.50   10.00

Poultry—Eggs (7.98)

Daily/Weekly Time Requirement (8.75)

Egg-laying hens and even ducks (although with less emphasis) are somewhat self-sufficient when the flock is small enough for the family (ten to twenty hens) and when they have an acre or more to roam. If they are restricted to a chicken run, then more supplemental feed will be required as their foraging capacity for insects, worms, plants, or compost is limited. With a simple watering system (five-gallon bucket) on a float switch and some space to roam, daily chores are limited to less than ten minutes a day: collecting eggs, observing the health of the flock, feeding kitchen scraps, and topping off feed and water.

Start-Up Expense (8.5)

There is some variance in the start-up expense based on whether you start with chicks or more mature birds. However, with a little handy work, some salvaging, and creativity, you can build a simple chicken coup and purchase fifteen chicks for less than five hundred dollars. Chicks are typically less than five dollars for common productive breeds like the Rhode Island Red and twenty to twenty-five dollars a hen for productive birds in their prime.

Family Friendliness (9.35)

Hens are typically very friendly, and the more they are handled, the friendlier they become. They are also small enough that they rarely provide any threat to children. Note: roosters in the flock can be a mixed bag with small children, as some of them can become aggressive and peck or scratch children. We have had one or two roosters in the past that, for whatever reason, felt threatened by our children and spurred a child. When this has happened, we would cull them immediately and turn them into coq au vin for dinner. Most of our roosters (we figure one per ten to twelve hens), however, have not been an issue. The main benefit to having roosters is they provide some level of protection to the hens (hence the spurring incident) and they fertilize the eggs if you are wanting to incubate and hatch your own eggs at some point.

Cash Value to Family (5)

At our current feed prices in the South for nonorganic feed and free-ranging the chickens, our cost to produce a dozen eggs is approximately $1.50–1.80 a dozen, and to buy the same product in the store would cost us about $8 a dozen with our post-income tax salary or nearly $9–10 of pre-tax income. When figuring the true costs in that manner, we are saving $7–8 a dozen for high-quality eggs, $35–40 a week, and $1,800–2,000 a year by raising our own if figuring five dozen eggs a week.

Learning Curve (9.5)

Chickens are pretty straightforward. If you provide food, water, and shelter from bad weather and predators, keep their space sanitary with either deep bedding or rotated on fresh pasture, and the majority of issues with chickens (smells, flies, and disease) are kept at bay. Hens are most productive from about nine months of age until eighteen months of age, so if you are wanting to keep your flock young and productive, it will require keeping track of their age (loosely place a different color zip tie around the feet of hens the same age) and cull (kill) the old hens. Culled hens are excellent as stew birds for chicken broth but are not as pleasant to eat as chicken meat from the store. Many new homesteaders do not bother with this management method. However, as the flock ages and egg production dwindles, it usually catches the attention of the resident chef.

Acreage Requirements (10)

Chickens are only second to bees or rabbits when it comes to production footprints. Many cities and townships across the country over the past decade have relaxed restrictions on having a small flock of hens (no roosters), and many families have discovered the joy and abundance of backyard chickens. So they can be kept to about two to three square feet per hen; however, our preference (if space allows) is to have a roaming flock to improve the diet and health of the birds and minimize outside inputs, which add expense.

Seasonal Variance (2.75)

There is little seasonal variance with managing hens in the South. If you live in a cold weather climate with prolonged snow and sub-freezing weather, providing adequate warm and dry space for them will be necessary. Providing the basics of food and water does not change, but it's worth noting that egg production waxes and wanes based on molting (seasonal feather replacement) and available daylight. When determining the size of your flock, we figure out how many eggs we need weekly, then double the flock size based on a mature and productive hen producing one egg a day. By using this formula, we tend to come out with our needs on average during the lower production times of the year, and in the peak production when there is a flush of eggs, we have a surplus to barter with, preserve, or enjoy more quiche or frittatas.

Production Expense (7)

The ongoing expense of chickens is almost entirely feed. A small flock of hens, if left to free range or to a large movable enclosure (electrified netting), can forage for most of their diet. They will still need some supplemental grain and they also make good use of kitchen scraps, especially any used eggshells for the calcium. Regular rotation also diminishes the buildup of things like mites. There is always debate about organic versus nonorganic feed, so expenses can vary. We find the best value for the highest quality product is to use a conventional all-stock feed. However, we provide an endless supply of organic greens, bugs, and kitchen leftovers to our pastured flock.

Harvest Requirement (10)

There is nothing simpler than egg collecting, especially for children. A simple wicker basket in hand when you go to feed scraps gets the job done. If you decide to expand the flock to more than a dozen hens or so, having some nesting boxes does help simplify that harvest process and keep the eggs cleaner, minimizing the time to clean them inside. Typically, we do not wash the eggs until prior to use or selling or bartering with friends as this keeps the eggs shelf stable for a longer period of time at room temperature.

Bartering Value (6)

In light of the recent egg shortages we are seeing in 2022/2023, eggs have become an increased bartering tool, especially with friends and family who live in town where a dozen high-quality free-range eggs are now approaching double digits. Historically, however, eggs were a staple commodity and have been seen as of lower value primarily due to the perceived abundance and low cost of industrial egg production. That being said, once a pastured, free-range egg is compared to an industrial egg both in color and taste, good eggs should always command a strong means of exchange among those who appreciate quality in taste and nutrition. However, since so many people begin with hens, there are simply more of them in the bartering world.

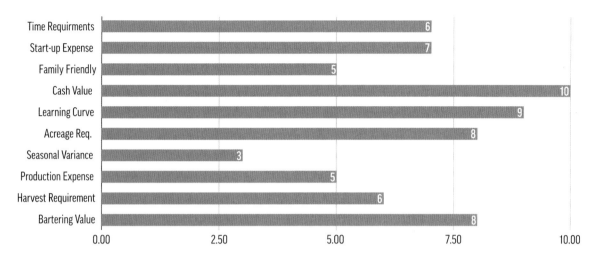

HOGS

Hogs (7.4)

Daily/Weekly Time Requirement (6)

Hogs, like most livestock, require daily attention. The size of the animal and the growth rate can often catch a new homesteader off guard if their infrastructure (fencing/water is not properly set up the first time. Hogs can be disrupting their infrastructure and a drain on time if they are constantly escaping. However, if the time/research is taken to establish a proper fencing and a watering system the daily routine of growing a small drove of pigs is very feasible.

Start-Up Expense (7)

Depending on the style of pens or paddocks, hogs can vary in start-up costs. Inexpensive electric fences and netting can be used to great effect and are cheaper than hard fences, but electric fencing has the added expense of a fence charger. The piglets themselves can run from under one hundred dollars to hundreds, depending on breed, size, and so on. Other infrastructure can be salvaged from old fifty-five-gallon drums cut in half for water or food. Most feed stores carry new feed troughs, but they come at a higher price.

Family Friendliness (5)

Piglets are very cute and even workable. There's a reason some people keep them as pets, but there are better reasons to keep them for meat. That being said, as pigs get larger, they present more danger from their sheer size and sometimes aggressiveness, and they tend to use up their time like a guest that has stayed too long so that when it is time to harvest the meat, you are ready for them to go.

Cash Value to Family (10)

Pork is cheap in the store, but its quality is often so low that it is hard to compare with fresh farm-raised pork. Harvesting a whole hog also has the added benefit of all of the special cuts, like lard fat, bacon, and other roasts. Therefore, the value is very high for the family, especially because the sheer abundance of a single hog is so great and the time to raise them is relatively short compared to other livestock, like cows.

Learning Curve (9)

Hogs are pretty simple and durable. Caring for them is not much more complicated than feeding and watering, depending on the style of growing them. Very few people have trouble with keeping hogs, even their first time. The simplest point of entry is to start with some feeder piglets that are castrated and grow them out to about 200–250 pounds for slaughter. Keeping and breeding pigs adds additional complexities to the management of this enterprise and can quickly become overwhelming, especially if multiple sows are being bred.

Acreage Requirements (8)

Hogs stink when they are in small pens. This can be mitigated, however, by either having a constant addition of bedding or simply rotating them or even cleaning out the pen. This is easier than it sounds because, despite ideas to the contrary, hogs are very orderly animals in that they like to designate specific places for eating, pooping, and sleeping, so you know where the stink is coming from. With larger or rotated pens, the ick factor can go away almost completely. Hogs also have the added benefit of being able to be pastured in the woods, allowing them to forage and even clean out wooded areas. Training hogs to mind an electric fence does take some effort and time, but doing so will expand your options for new locations and allow you to benefit from their tilling instinct.

Seasonal Variance (3)

If you let your hogs forage or rotate them through paddocks, there is more work in bringing them to the food. If, however, you bring the food to them in purchased feeds, then the variance is very little. Hogs can be raised in about six months to a harvestable weight, so there can be breaks in the management of this enterprise.

Production Expense (5)

There are ways to greatly lower the ongoing cost of feed by utilizing scraps and other food waste. Many families have a hog just for this purpose, as the hog captures any waste from food and turns it into more food. One of our priests grew up collecting stale bread and other waste from his local grocery to eliminate his feed bill for the family hogs. Outside of collecting slop, the quality and expense of feed will depend on the presence and products of local mills.

Harvest Requirement (6)

Harvest requirements for a hog are largely determined by skills and comfort levels. Unlike smaller animals, like rabbits, butchering a hog is quite an affair. For this reason, hog-killing is both seasonal and communal; it's enjoyable and a good time to do with others. For many, however, you will need the help of a seasoned butcher or even a meat processing plant, which is added time and expense.

Bartering Value (8)

Because quality pork is relatively hard to find, owing to the poor quality of industrialized pork, those that know and want good meat will respect a high bartering value for the hog. Also, if you are raising one, you might as well raise more if you have the room, and then a whole hog can be set aside for larger bartering needs like skilled services or craftsmen.

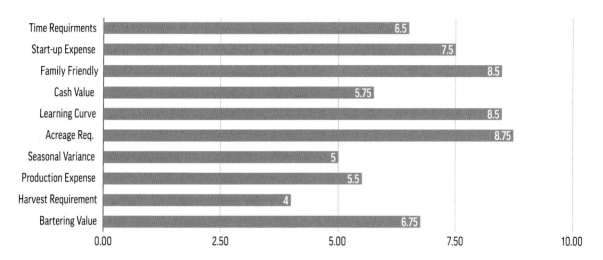

PASTURED POULTRY - FRYER

	Value
Time Requirments	6.5
Start-up Expense	7.5
Family Friendly	8.5
Cash Value	5.75
Learning Curve	8.5
Acreage Req.	8.75
Seasonal Variance	5
Production Expense	5.5
Harvest Requirement	4
Bartering Value	6.75

Pastured Poultry—Fryer (7.01)

Daily/Weekly Time Requirement (6.5)

Pastured poultry is a daily chore. Usually, they are grown in large batches (50–100+), which means that rotating them to fresh pasture or cleaning their housing is a daily chore that must be done without question. However, a run of meat birds are usually only on the farm for ten to twelve weeks, so this work is not constant in the way egg-layers are.

Start-Up Expense (7.5)

The cost of chicks is relatively low (four to five dollars), and movable chicken tractors can be made from scraps and salvaged materials. Even building from new materials can be relatively inexpensive. Other equipment can either be made or purchased, like water and food containers, so there is variance in overhead costs, but in general, one should be able to get into the enterprise for less than a thousand dollars (including the cost of birds for the first season).

Family Friendliness (8.5)

Like egg-layers, "broilers," or meat birds, are fun to watch and work with. Children can get involved much more easily. However, because pastured poultry is often around for shorter periods of time, there is less direct interaction with the kids. They aren't as pet-like as laying hens due to their disproportionate bodies (chicken breast, anyone?). The daily chores of feeding, watering, and moving to fresh pasture can also be a daily family endeavor.

Cash Value to Family (5.75)

Chicken from the supermarket is hard to compete with. Not only does industrial chicken generally have a respectable taste, but it is also cheap due to the insane economies of scale the industrial farms run. Of course, we must consider that the quality and taste of pastured birds is much greater, not to mention pastured broilers are arguably raised in a more humane manner and the need for coccidiostats or antibiotics are non-existent. When we compare our cost of feed, starter chicks, and a 10 percent mortality rate (but not our labor), we come out to about five to seven dollars cheaper per bird compared to a certified organic/free range chicken from the store and about the equivalent price for a conventional factory farmed chicken.

Learning Curve (8.5)

Like laying hens, daily attention to food and water is necessary and mitigates most issues. Unlike laying hens though, most meat birds are run in smaller (10' x 10') movable spaces to protect them from predators, keep their meat more tender (limit running), and focus the foraging to a specific space. Given their relatively small size, it isn't hard to learn how to handle a flock of meat birds. The most intensive and sensitive time, however, is in the early stage when chicks need to be brooded with heat lamps in indoor, protected areas.

Acreage Requirements (8.75)

If one has a small plot of grass, a rotating group of meat birds can keep a small lawn mowed (or, rather, they turn mowing into a real value). The enterprise can be easily scaled up or down depending on the needs of the family and the availability of land. Joel Salatin, the icon of pastured poultry, routinely runs up to five hundred birds per acre per season.

Seasonal Variance (5)

As mentioned above, meat birds are a short-term endeavor because they are rarely on the farm for more than twelve weeks, making this enterprise easy to turn on or off. Many homesteaders will run one or two batches (50–100+ birds) in the spring to fill the freezer for the year and then be done with pastured poultry. It is best to run them once the weather has stabilized (late spring, summer, fall) and the threat of severe cold is not a concern. In the Deep South, many producers take the summer months (July, August) off because the intense heat and humidity can cause increased mortality to the flock.

Production Expense (5.5)

Like other livestock, the presence and specifics (organic vs. conventional) of the feed vary greatly. Meat birds cannot live off kitchen scraps and foraging; they require a steady, high-protein diet. However, keeping these birds on daily fresh pasture will help reduce your feed bill by up to 30 percent. Even still, it's unbelievable how much food the standard broiler (CornishxRock) consumes in the last two to three weeks of their lives as they are genetically selected to grow fast, gain weight, and almost be immobile near harvest. There are more versatile and natural breeds, like the Rhode Island Reds; however, their dressed carcass is significantly smaller than what we have become accustomed to in the store.

Harvest Requirement (4)

Although not as easy as rabbits due to the difficulty of removing the feathers, which require the skill of scalding and plucking, chickens can be harvested at the homestead. If you plan to do more than a couple of birds each year, an electric chicken plucking machine is highly recommended (which runs around five hundred dollars) as well as several kill cones and an efficient way of scalding the birds. Rarely do people pay to have them processed (although this is a possibility if you lack the time or skill). There is no benefit to holding onto meat birds for more than twelve weeks as their weight gain peaks but the high food consumption remains never-ending, so when it is time for them to go, it is time for them to go.

Bartering Value (6.75)

Because most are not opposed to the taste of store-bought chicken and the price from the store is very hard to compete with, the bartering value is only so-so. However, a deal can still be struck with those who are more conscious of the quality of a pastured hen.

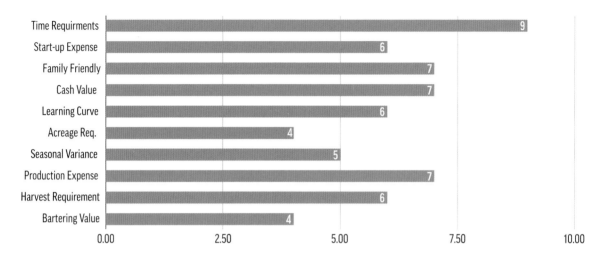

SHEEP

Sheep (6.45)

Daily/Weekly Time Requirement (9)

Like most livestock, there is a need for regular attention to sheep. However, because they are grazing animals, it is not nearly as demanding as something like hogs or rabbits, simply because they harvest their own food. They can be managed/trained on electric fencing and can also be run on less-established pasture (they can handle a bit of brush). We only run hair sheep, and they do not need sheering, so we do not have experience with that aspect.

Start-Up Expense (6)

If you have existing infrastructure for other animals—fencing, pasture, and water—sheep can be a low-cost addition to other enterprises and work well with them since, for example, they tend to graze different species in the same pasture as cows.

Family Friendliness (7)

Sheep are cute and small. The risk of any injury is much smaller and probably limited to males ramming children. They can be more skittish, so handling them may be rarer, but they are beautiful and docile in general.

Cash Value to Family (7)

Fresh lamb for Easter has tremendous value. And because it is less common in the United States, having lamb and mutton can be a great value and bring variety to the standard American diet. There are even cost savings from not having to run a mower or tractor; sheep, once trained to fencing, can be very beneficial.

Learning Curve (6)

Some sheep species are higher maintenance than others, but in general, if you find the breeds that are lower maintenance, sheep are great entry-level mid-size livestock. In general, they are more prone to parasites if not properly de-wormed on a regular basis and or managed properly (rotational grazing). If space allows, rotating sheep and cows in the same area can be mutually beneficial as the parasites do not cross over to the different species, and sheep like the woody brush that cows do not.

Acreage Requirements (4)

Sheep require pasture. Since they are smaller, naturally this is on the lower end of pasture needs as opposed to something like cows. The general rule of thumb is seven sheep eat the same amount of pasture as one cow. In our area, we can typically run seven sheep per acre and keep the pasture properly managed. Though this is subjective to each location, annual rainfall, and season. It's best to check with the county extension service for local suggestions on animal density per acre.

Seasonal Variance (5)

Through the grazing seasons, there will be very little variance in work, and the primary variance will be if they are housed and fed with hay during the dormant growing seasons. Learning to manage your pasture takes time, knowledge, and some money. It's possible in the southern half of the country to extend the pasture by overlapping different species of grass that thrive in both cool weather and warm or hot weather.

Production Expense (7)

Once the pasture is established, a well-maintained field will minimize the cost of keeping sheep. As mentioned prior, depending on your density and rotation program, a dewormer may also be necessary. Providing food (hay or grain) in the offseason is also a consideration.

Harvest Requirement (6)

Larger than rabbits and chickens but smaller than pigs and cattle, harvesting sheep is still a considerable amount of work (equivalent to a smaller deer). Most homesteaders in America do not raise them for the fur, but if you wanted, this would require another set of skills and tools (beyond our experience). Sometimes it can be hard to find meat processing facilities that are interested in sheep because of their small size and lower return per animal, so learning to do it or finding someone to come to you may be more pressing than with hogs or cows.

Bartering Value (4)

While sheep are not common to the average American, there is a strong market for live sheep among the Muslim and Hispanic communities. One thing to note is that if you plan to sell live sheep to the Muslims, they only buy unblemished lambs (i.e., not castrated).

GOATS

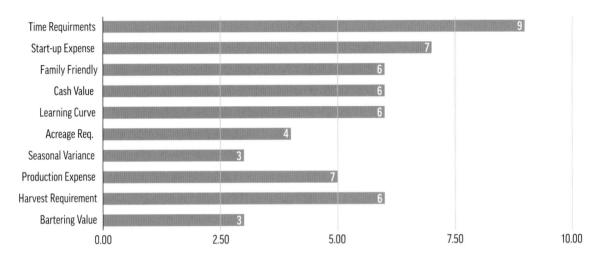

Goats (6)

Daily/Weekly Time Requirement (9)

Like other ruminants, once the proper infrastructure is set up, there is little that requires daily attention outside of providing water and sufficient food (pasture, brush,
or grain). Goats, however, are known for their crafty ability to get through fencing
and are more difficult to train to electric fencing than sheep or cows. If one plans to
milk goats (Nubian is the most preferred breed), it's worth handling them daily and
training them to eat (before they freshen up) in their stanchions. Every six to eight
weeks, you will need to trim the hooves to maintain proper health and minimize injury and infection.

Start-Up Expense (7)

Most goats run for two to three hundred dollars apiece; however, you can often find a
homesteader or homeowner who is at their wit's end with escaping goats and willing to
offer a bargain. You'll need a simple shed and a milking stanchion if you plan to go that
route. It's worth not skimping on fencing for the goats and using four- to five-foot tall
woven wire attached to posts and pulled taught.

Family Friendliness (6)

Most daily goat chores can be handled by children age six or older (feed and water); however, trimming hooves is recommended to be done by adolescents and adults on the homestead as they have to be held somewhat still and trimmed with hoof shears. Our eight- and ten-year-olds milk Nubian goats without issue; they are much less intimidating than a Jersey cow.

Cash Value to Family (6)

Goat milk, cheese, and other dairy products, as well as soaps, are probably the most common in America. However, goat meat, or chevon, is increasingly more common in the United States, especially in niche markets. Chevon, like mutton (sheep), does have a unique taste, but most people find it agreeable.

Learning Curve (6)

Goats, similar to sheep, are relatively easy to care for if the basics of food, water, and shelter are provided. Like the other ruminants, they are prone to parasites and will need to be treated (oral or drench). Rotating them to new areas helps with this; however, due to the fencing requirements, goats can be more costly compared to rotating sheep or cows.

Acreage Requirements (4)

Goats handle pasture, brush, and even dense forest well. Many use them to clear the understory or abandoned farmland because they are so versatile. That being said, they do need space, and once they have consumed the greenery in their area, they will either need to be moved or feed will need to be brought in.

Season Variance (3)

There is little variance in care from season to season other than providing food, water, and shelter.

Production Expense (7)

The day-to-day expense of goats can be relatively minimal if they graze for their food. It's worth providing mineral blocks to supplement their diet, but they can usually be shared with the other ruminants.

Harvest Requirement (6)

Milking Nubians is relatively simple and requires only a simple milking stanchion, bucket, and other sanitary care, similar to cows. The slaughter of a goat is comparable to a deer (in size), and it can easily be handled on the homestead. It's worth aging the meat in a cooler or, if done in a colder climate, it can be dry aged outside with a damp sheet wrapped around it in the winter.

Bartering Value (3)

Dairy products and soap are fairly mainstream and carry strong bartering values. Goat meat is not as common but is growing in demand in the United States, especially among Indian immigrants, who are used to enjoying the Burger King Whopper made with goat meat!

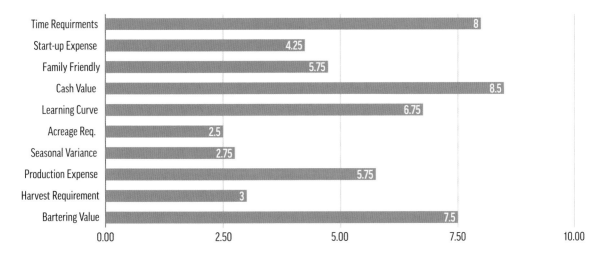

CATTLE - BEEF

Time Requirments	8
Start-up Expense	4.25
Family Friendly	5.75
Cash Value	8.5
Learning Curve	6.75
Acreage Req.	2.5
Seasonal Variance	2.75
Production Expense	5.75
Harvest Requirement	3
Bartering Value	7.5

Cattle—Beef (5.9)

Daily/Weekly Time Requirement (8)

Cattle are often seen in the countryside because they don't require much work. Depending on the style of grazing, you can either just put them out to pasture and come get them when they're done or work with them daily through intensive (rotational) grazing. The latter is significantly better for the land and parasite load, but it is considerably more work.

Start-Up Expense (4.25)

Depending on the size of the land and the current state of the pasture, fencing, water, and seed for the pasture can be a considerable expense. The largest expense outside of the infrastructure will be the cows. Starting out, it's recommended for a smaller homestead to buy heifers (unbred females) or steers (castrated bulls) as they are generally easier to manage.

Family Friendliness (4.75)

It is said that cows are the number one killer of people on the homestead in America. This might be hard to believe, but if you ask farmers, they'll tell you to be careful with kids around them. While they are very docile and even easy to work with (they can be borderline pets), they are still very large, so if something goes wrong, it can go very wrong.

Cash Value to Family (8.5)

Although the taste of beef from the store can be decent, farm-raised beef has an excellent taste and is significantly healthier. In fact, when people speak of red meat as being unhealthy, rarely is the data examined about grass-fed beef. And the sheer quantity of a finished cow makes the value higher since you get every cut for the same price as something like ground or stew beef.

Learning Curve (6.75)

Working with cattle requires patience, docility, and a certain level of confidence. Having good infrastructure (perimeter fencing) helps with the latter, as does handling them regularly. In addition to managing the pasture and watching their rumen (a part of the stomach you can observe externally that indicates food availability) and body weight, most conventional cattle farmers deworm their cattle on a regular basis, although those who rotate their livestock daily see a significantly lower parasite load and debate the use of deworming.

Acreage Requirements (2.5)

Cows need pasture and require the most land from the homestead. They can be utilized for other areas—like browsing in woods and cutover land—but they still generally need a couple of acres even for one cow, and that can be pushing it in some parts of the country due to the variance in the quality of the pasture and average rainfall. Greg Judy is a seasoned cattleman who provides good technical detail on laying out a grazing operation even for a small-scale homestead.

Seasonal Variance (2.75)

The seasonal variance of cows tends to sway between grazing seasons and hay seasons. During grazing (late spring, summer, and fall), time is spent rotating the animals from one paddock to the next, and during hay season (winter), the more cows you have, the more often you will have to feed hay.

Production Expense (5.75)

When they are fed high-quality grass, cow expense is very low. This is the great benefit of cows: they convert an uneatable resource (grass) into something palatable for humans. While there are all sorts of inputs that people might sell you, generally minerals are the only ongoing expense during growing seasons, assuming you have your pasture established. That being said, hay can be very expensive depending on the variety and your location. This expense can add up quickly in the winter since cows cannot be without food for extended periods. Their rumen needs to be full at all times, especially in the winter since this helps them stay warm. A tidbit on buying hay in round bales: beware of the diameter as not all balers are the same. A 4′ x 4′ bale has half the amount of hay that a 5′ x 5′ bale does!

Harvest Requirement (3)

The sheer size of cows makes their harvest a challenge, and the meat needs to be refrigerated for ten to fourteen days. While butchering a beef cow can be done at home, the cuts of beef are also harder to identify in the carcass compared to something like a pig, which has more recognizable cuts. Most people will opt for a meat processor, and those can vary greatly in availability, price, and proximity. Currently, our local custom butcher is booked for eighteen months!

Bartering Value (7.5)

Everyone loves a good steak, and slapping one down on the table in negotiations can go a long way. Due to their size, you can often afford to raise a cow and sell or barter half a cow to another family to help offset your production expense.

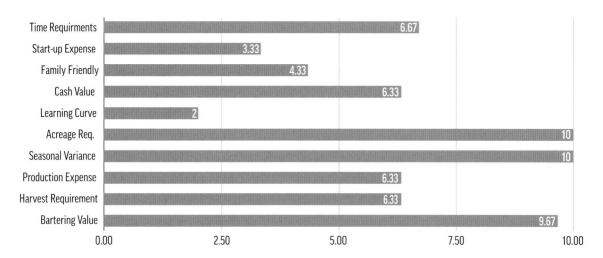

BEES

Category	Value
Time Requirments	6.67
Start-up Expense	3.33
Family Friendly	4.33
Cash Value	6.33
Learning Curve	2
Acreage Req.	10
Seasonal Variance	10
Production Expense	6.33
Harvest Requirement	6.33
Bartering Value	9.67

Beekeeping (5.5)

Daily/Weekly Time Requirement (6.67)

A lot of the daily and weekly time requirements for a small apiary of bees (less than ten colonies) change from season to season. In general, during the season, a good rule of thumb is to spend about thirty to sixty minutes working on bee-related things every seven to ten days. This can vary from working on equipment to inspecting colonies to treating for parasites to feeding supplements in the fall. However, some times of the year will require more attention.

Start-Up Expense (3.33)

Unless you are an avid woodworker, beekeeping will require a fair investment in woodenware (boxes, frames, lids, bottom board, etc.). It's typically figured one complete hive will cost around five hundred dollars, including the cost of the bees. This does not include the protective gear ($200+), hand tools (smoker $50, hive tool $10, dolly $150), or the harvesting extractor ($500–$1000+). There are also numerous labor-saving devices that are worthwhile if one plans to scale the endeavor beyond a couple of hives, but they aren't necessary. It's worth befriending a local beekeeper for the mentorship, and they also may know of a retiring beekeeper (or failed enterprise) that is having a fire sale on all the necessary equipment to make a start.

Family Friendliness (4.33)

Bee stings are the biggest limitation for family involvement in the craft. Some can tolerate the discomfort of the occasional sting, while others have no interest or may even be allergic. Other than working with the bees, there are other ways to include children in beekeeping, including extracting and bottling the honey, building the beehives in the woodshop, or molding the wax into candles.

Cash Value to Family (6.33)

If you can keep your bees alive (30 percent loss is the national average) and you are homesteading in an area where you can make an average sixty-pound surplus of honey per colony per year (which is more common in the eastern two-thirds of the country), typically one can pay for the initial investment plus the annual operating expense within two years. Obviously, if you experience colony loss (which is more common for new beekeepers) or make less than sixty pounds per hive, it will take longer to pay off the investment. Once the investment is paid off, and based on the sixty-pound average, you can figure a beekeeper can make a pound of honey for about one dollar, not including his labor or any other capital expenditures.

Learning Curve (2)

Beekeeping is extremely laborious and requires a fairly large knowledge base on the biology of bees, varroa mites (the primary lethal pest), local blooming flowers, and climate. The learning curve compared to other endeavors is rather steep. Prior to the 1990s, beekeepers could set out queen-right colonies with sufficient space to gather the honey crop and come back months later to harvest the honey. Today, unfortunately, bees require more intervention due to increased disease, pesticides, and insecticides. Hives are usually inspected and managed accordingly every ten to fourteen days during the season (spring, summer, and early fall).

Acreage Requirements (10)

The actual footprint of a bee colony is only 16" x20"; however, these welcomed trespassers will forage out up to three miles from their colony, so it is not absolutely necessary to have all the blooming forage on your own property, especially if you are adjacent to native grasslands, forests, or even agricultural fields. Most of the honey in the eastern part of the United States comes from wild trees like Maple, Poplar, Gum, or Basswood, so don't forget to look up when scouting for flowers.

Seasonal Variance (10)

Beekeeping is extremely variable with regard to the seasons. Generally, in the winter, time is spent building new bee boxes, repairing equipment, bottling any surplus honey from the prior season (for barter or sale), and processing beeswax for candles or other crafts. It is also a good time of year to plan for any additional needs in the spring (e.g., purchase of bees or equipment from other beekeepers). Spring needs vary from week to week based on what the flowers and weather are doing. Checking to make sure bees are not starving is usually required on the first warm (50°F+) day, providing food if need be. That transitions to treating for varroa mites, providing bees with enough space, and managing the colony to ensure it does not become overcrowded and swarm later in the spring. As spring transitions to summer, most healthy colonies begin storing a surplus of honey and will require more space for the incoming nectar. Once the nectar is completely ripened into honey, the honey harvest begins, and honey supers with the combs are collected and brought to a dedicated space for extraction and straining. Due to the mess of the process, it's ideal to have a separate space like a small shed or cleaned-up garage. Late summer and early fall usually require treating the colonies for mites (if not sooner) and then preparing the colonies for winter, which varies significantly based on latitude and elevation. It's best to consult your local beekeeping associate for the local knowledge needed to successfully navigate the craft.

Production Expense (6.33)

Once the initial investment is made in the beehives and associated equipment, a beekeeper can expect to purchase mite treatment (Oxalic Acid, Thymol, Formic Acid, or amitraz) for multiple treatments each year. Ideally, bees can provide enough stores of honey for themselves; however, if the weather does not cooperate (more common than

not), supplemental feeding with sugar syrup may be necessary. Feeding starving bees is an act of charity! It's also highly recommended to "re-queen" each colony annually with a young queen. This helps reduce the risk of swarming and also increases the odds of making it through to the following year. All these expenses can add up to somewhere in the ballpark of fifty-sixty dollars or more per year, per colony.

Harvest Requirement (6.33)

Harvesting honey at the homestead for two to ten colonies can be accomplished with a dolly, a fume board, and a bee blower. Once the bees are removed from the honey supers and moved back to your honey house and extractor (in a bee-free enclosure), the honey is typically spun out using centrifugal force. If one only has a couple of boxes to harvest, then the crush and strain method is an option and only requires a couple of five-gallon buckets, cheesecloth (or equivalent), and some patience. Cut-comb is another extractor-free option but requires a different management strategy and configuration that is beyond the scope of this overview.

Bartering Value (9.67)

Honey, similar to maple syrup, is highly desirable and an excellent product to barter with. It is one of the crafts that does not take that much more overhead after the initial investment to scale from a couple of hives to ten hives, but the output can increase significantly (from 120 pounds to 600 pounds). The concern about bee stings, the learning curve, and the cost of entry also keep many people from pursuing the craft, so the demand for local honey and beeswax candles still exceeds the supply in most locations.

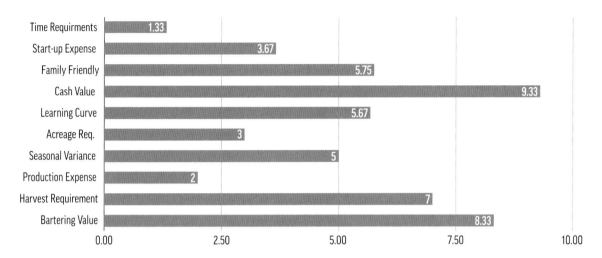

CATTLE - DAIRY

	Value
Time Requirments	1.33
Start-up Expense	3.67
Family Friendly	5.75
Cash Value	9.33
Learning Curve	5.67
Acreage Req.	3
Seasonal Variance	5
Production Expense	2
Harvest Requirement	7
Bartering Value	8.33

Cattle—Dairy (5.5)

Daily/Weekly Time Requirement (1.33)

There are few things as demanding as a family milk cow. Unlike beef cows, they are either brought in daily from the pasture or kept in a barn, which is more maintenance. And milking them is not optional; missing a milking or milking poorly can cause infection and other problems.

Start-Up Expense (3.67)

The expense is based on infrastructure and milking systems. If you are hand-milking, the only requirement is a decent bucket. Automatic bucket-milker systems are more expensive, and larger pipeline systems, which are the cleanest and most efficient, are often cost-prohibitive for the average homesteader. Although cows can be milked out in the field, it is highly recommended that there be a clean and dry place for this regular chore.

Family Friendliness (5.75)

Milk cows can be very sweet and enjoyable for children. Kids often become part of the milking process since it includes things like putting out feed and even bottle-feeding calves. However, cows are still large and dangerous animals. A child who is unaware or complacent may find himself kicked or knocked around by a cow eager to get to her feed or suffering from an unseen injury. Milk cows are, therefore, great for a family but require diligence.

Cash Value to Family (9.33)

The value of a milk cow is in both the abundance and the potential variety. Milk has many value-added products that can be made: cheese, butter, kefir, yogurt, ice cream, and so on. Therefore, the value is very high, and it can be a central source of food for the family, which is why the old advocacy that each man needs three acres and a cow was so common. And because most people breed their cows once a year, they produce meat for the family. They also provide manure for the garden.

Learning Curve (5.67)

Handling a milk cow requires either good experience and endurance or an already docile and easy cow (i.e., pre-trained to be milked). Very often, the hardest part of learning to milk cows is the beginning, when the effort it actually takes to milk them can be shocking at first, although after a while, it settles into a simple routine.

Acreage Requirements (3)

Like beef cows, milk cows need grass daily. Many people, however, successfully keep barn cows if they don't have pasture. This requires even more work and the input of purchased hay, but the amazing amount of milk and compost it provides is often seen as worth it.

Seasonal Variance (5)

Milking is a daily chore, but there are rest periods when you dry up a cow before calving. You can also move to milking once a day (as opposed to the more common twice a day) a couple of months after calving.

Production Expense (2)

Ongoing expense is tied to hay and feed. Most dairy cows have been bred to require the input of grain, which also serves as the most common means of enticing them into the milking area. Like other feeds, this expense will be related to the availability and quality of local feeds.

Harvest Requirement (7)

Harvesting milk is constant. It definitely becomes a dominating aspect of homesteading. If you have a single person milking, then hand-milking is usually sufficient. However, unless you are milking daily, the habit and muscles often don't develop enough to make this doable in a way that keeps the cow milked out and happy. Therefore, if you are rotating or sharing the chore of milking, it is more likely that you will need to have an automatic milker of some sort, which adds time to the chore—mostly the time it takes to clean the equipment.

Bartering Value (8.33)

Raw milk and other dairy products are highly valued by those that know about their benefits. And since not everyone has the time or willingness to milk a cow every day, raw milk is not as plentiful as something like eggs (many people have chickens), so it commands a good exchange.

LUMBER & FOREST PRODUCTS

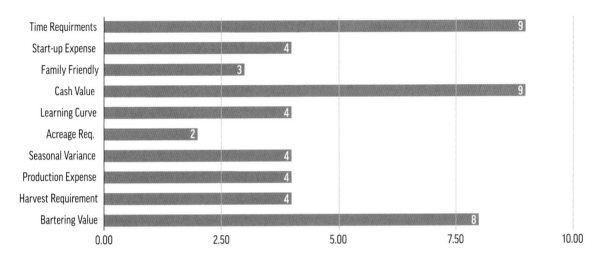

Timber and Forest Products (5.45)

Daily/Weekly Time Requirement (9)

Harvesting from the forest can take as much time as you need or as little. With a healthy stand of trees, you can produce lumber and firewood, and intertwine it with other endeavors, like growing or foraging for mushrooms, running hogs during the acorn harvest, or foraging for other roots and grubs.

Start-Up Expense (4)

Given that access to land is secured, the expense of harvesting from the woods is almost entirely in the equipment you use. At a minimum, chainsaws are often employed, though there are some that reserve with reverence the right to rigor in hand saws and axes. Larger equipment, like sawmills, do not necessarily have to be owned because there are often local mills, and even traveling ones, that can turn trees into lumber for you. However, if one has the time and money, the presence of a mill can add much to a homestead's resources.

Family Friendliness (3)

The woods can be magical. There is great satisfaction in getting to know and managing a healthy timber stand. However, the work of a sawyer often has the danger of heavy equipment and falling trees, which is not suited for younger kids if done on any scale.

Cash Value to Family (9)

Wood is historically cheap, but that can change quickly. Although firewood is relatively cheap, if one is heating with it exclusively, the work done to procure it yourself saves a lot of money. Lumber can also be of a higher quality and provide satisfaction.

Learning Curve (4)

Working with wood can seem easy, but without proper training and experience, cutting down trees can be dangerous (even deadly) and frustrating—for example, when dealing with dull chains, bound saws, poorly dropped trees, and so on. With some training and time, it becomes intuitive work, but without that, it can be a challenge. Running a mill is also not for the faint of heart or mechanically inexperienced. Regular maintenance, repairs, and constant observation of the work at hand is needed. As one local sawyer likes to remind me, "I looked away for a split second, and now look at my hand!" Once the lumber is rough cut, the drying and planning is a whole other process that takes considerable time, attention, knowledge, and equipment.

Acreage Requirements (2)

Trees only demand the soil they grow in. If you are harvesting mainly from your own land, then this is a renewable resource (especially on a decadal scale), but it requires care and attention to present and future needs. Trees don't grow in a day, so giving time and space is necessary. However, you can often find access to woodlots for little to no cost, depending on what you are harvesting.

Seasonal Variance (4)

Although trees can be harvested at any time, working in the woods during cooler and winter months is common to avoid things like wasp nests and even snakes. That being said, working with wood serves as a filler job when other enterprises are less demanding.

Production Expense (4)

The ongoing expense is, again, primarily in the maintenance and fuel of equipment. If you are using diesel or gas, therefore, your expenses are dependent on the global economy, and in this way, there is less independence and more potential for unexpected increases. However, a chainsaw, for its output, is probably one of the most efficient tools on the homestead that uses fossil fuels.

Harvest Requirement (4)

As mentioned above, harvesting is a matter of tools, time, and skill level. At a minimum, felling a tree requires a saw, safety gear, and a way to move the downed tree once cut into desirable sections. It's a good rule of thumb to over-cut the log by one to two feet per section for the desirable rough-cut lumber length to accommodate for shrinkage, split ends, and so on.

Bartering Value (8)

A barn full of seasoned firewood or lumber can be something highly valued in bartering, especially if people care about quality and species, like fine woodworkers. Lumber in large lumber yards and big box stores has decreased significantly in quality over the years, and better wood is more appreciated by artisan woodworkers.

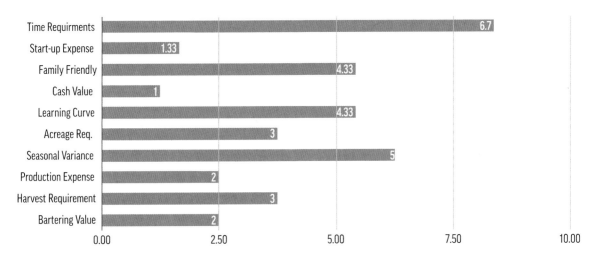

EQUINE

Equine (3.15)

Daily/Weekly Time Requirement (6.7)

Horses typically require feeding two times a day in addition to hay and/or pasture. Feed requirements vary from horse to horse but the saying "eating like a horse" exists for a reason. Their feet need trimming every five to six weeks, which is usually outsourced to a farrier. Those who show horses and have bits in their horses' mouths frequently require regular dental work as well. For the homestead where they are either used for labor or as pets, one could forgo the dental care. If you truly plan to use them for labor or transportation around the homestead, they will require regular handling and training.

Start-Up Expense (1.33)

Outside of the fencing, pasture, water, and the stable, which can overlap with other enterprises, the cost of a respectable horse without major physical or mental issues will run five thousand dollars and up. Be wary of any deals as some dishonest horsemen may drug a bad horse so it acts calm in order to get rid of it, only for a family to have a nightmare on their hands. It's worth having an experienced handler to assist in the procuring of a horse if you are a rookie.

Family Friendliness (4.33)

In the riding community, most children do not consistently ride horses until age seven or eight for the obvious reason that they are big animals. Temperament, personality, and how they are kept will determine how friendly the horse is as well.

Cash Value to Family (1)

From a homesteading perspective in the twenty-first century, horses are just an expense. Americans don't eat horses, and they don't produce any material good for the family. However, in the event of a catastrophic disaster where vehicles are useless, they could serve as a means of transportation and labor around the farm. Generally speaking though, horses are bought today as a hobby or for personal or emotional interest.

Learning Curve (4.33)

Handling horses is unlike other large livestock for the primary reason that usually one rides a horse. There is a great level of intuition needed to understand a horse and to properly handle and care for the animal. It's worth investing time and money into lessons even before buying a horse to gain this intuition and skill and see if the family and children are serious about such a large commitment.

Acreage Requirements (3)

While horses can be kept in a stable and then ridden, having them on pasture reduces parasite loads and, in general, improves behavior, especially for certain horses. You can even rotate pasture, similar to you would for cows and sheep, to help maintain better health for your horse and pasture.

Seasonal Variance (5)

Horses actually prefer cooler weather and do better in the fall and winter in most of the United States. Summer heat in the South can be oppressive and stressful for horses, and they are usually handled less during intense heat spells.

Production Expense (2)

Horse feed, vet bills, farrier bills, and dental bills: a horse is a lot to maintain for a leisurely ride.

Harvest Requirement (3)

This does not really apply to horses, but if you are planning to harvest their labor for a log harvest, plow, or carriage, the equipment (rope, bit, etc.) is simple, but the training and handling prior to the events will take time and a level of commitment above the occasional ride around the farm.

Bartering Value (2)

Again, outside of bartering its labor for horse lessons or pulling a plow or a carriage, the horse has essentially (in some eyes, sadly) been replaced by the tractor.

Jason M. Craig writes from a small dairy farm in Western NC. He is the co-founder of Fraternus, founding editor of *Sword & Spade* magazine, and author of *Leaving Boyhood Behind* and *The Traditional Virtues According* to *St. Thomas Aquinas: A Study for Men*. He holds a master's degree from the Augustine Institute and is known to claim his family invented bourbon.

Thomas D. Van Horn and his family have "lived off-the-land" in NW Florida over the past ten years by homesteading, keeping 400-600 bee colonies, and selling honey and beeswax candles.